CREATION
SPIRITUALITY
&
THE DREAMTIME

CREATION SPIRITUALITY & THE DREAMTIME

MATTHEW FOX

JOANNA MACY

VERONICA BRADY

KEVIN TRESTON

ELIZABETH CAIN

EDDIE KNEEBONE

Edited By
CATHERINE HAMMOND

MILLENNIUM
BOOKS

First published in 1991 by
Millennium Books, an imprint of
E. J. Dwyer (Australia) Pty Ltd
3/32–72 Alice Street
Newtown NSW 2042

National Library of Australia
Cataloguing-in-Publication data

Creation spirituality & the dreamtime.

ISBN 0 85574 364 6.
1. Spirituality. [2]. Aborigines, Australian – Religion.
3. Man – Influence on nature. I. Fox, Matthew, 1940–
II. Hammond, Catherine.

291.4

Text design: Katrina Rendell
Typeset in 11/13 Goudy by SRM Production Services Sdn.
Bhd. Malaysia.
Printed by SRM Production Services Sdn. Bhd. Malaysia.

Contents

Acknowledgments

The authors gratefully acknowledge permission to use material from the following works. Every effort has been made to locate the sources of quoted material and to obtain authorization for its use.

The Great Cosmic Mother: Rediscovering the Religion of the Earth, Monica Sjoo and Barbara Mor, Harper San Francisco, copyright © 1987, Monica Sjoo and Barbara Mor.

Centuries of Meditation, Thomas Traherne, The Faith Press, London; Harper Collins, New York, 1960.

The Old Mendicant, Thich Nhat Hanh, Parallax Press, Berkeley, California.

Escape, D. H. Lawrence. Lawrence Pollinger Ltd., and the Estate of Frieda Lawrence Ravagli.

Remember the Tarantella, Fiona Moorhead, Primavera Press, Sydney, 1987.

Mysteries of the Dreaming, James Cowan, Prism Press, Bridport, Dorset, U.K., 1989.

The Songlines, Bruce Chatwin, Random Century, London, 1988.

My People, Oodgeroo of the tribe Noonuccal custodian of the land Minjerribah, Jacaranda Press Ltd. Aust., 1964.

About the Authors

MATTHEW FOX:
Dominican priest, Director of the Institute in Culture and Creation Spirituality, Oakland, California, author of thirteen books.

JOANNA MACY:
Author, popular speaker, adjunct professor at the California Institute of Integral Studies, Starr King School for the Ministry, Berkeley.

KEVIN TRESTON:
Author, specialist in leadership development and pastoral ministry, lecturer in adult education.

VERONICA BRADY:
A Loreto Sister, author, senior lecturer in English in the University of Western Australia.

ELIZABETH CAIN:
Lecturer, group facilitator, Jungian analyst, specialist in personal development and spirituality.

EDDIE KNEEBONE:

Promoter of an educational movement to disseminate appreciation of authentic Australian Aboriginal culture and spirituality.

Editor's Note

A most unconventional one...

Bringing this book together from the talks given at the 1990 Australian Creation Spirituality Workshop (LaTrobe University, Melbourne) could sound like a very detached and prosaic editing task. It was anything but!

It was an experience flooded by brilliant shafts of light bursting out everywhere, mind-boggling ideas from the near and far reaches of the universe. None of these remained mere surface thoughts — they all seemed to be finding a home in parts of my psyche heretofore unknown to me.

In such circumstances editing becomes anything but prosaic. I resonated, I pondered, I held my breath at the scope of experience, wisdom, wit and caring concern shown by all the contributors to the workshop and the book. To Eileen Marchmont and the other members of the Australian Friends of Creation, thanks are owed for creating the environment that nurtured the rich interraction this book reflects.

Unforgettable features are Matthew Fox's pithy reflections, many of them offered with tongue in cheek, such as: 'Everything is moving in the universe, everything is dancing the cosmic dance... except a few white Christians... in high places'; and 'We have inherited a dysfunctional Christianity'; and 'Most parents are given children as their spiritual directors'.

I found myself thinking in new ways after exposure to Matt's challenging fire. Nor am I the same person I was before I heard Joanna Macy proclaim: 'We stand and move with the full authority of our four-and-a-half-billion-year life!'

And when she says with characteristic conviction, 'Something in us wants to be born,' I know she is articulating what I've seen dancing on the fringe of my consciousness for a long time, a sense of something unknown but beautiful that is waiting to be born. And now this volume proclaims that my experience is part of the new Unitary Age, this birthing universe so named by Kevin Treston. Something, somewhere, everywhere, is about to burst forth. You can feel it in the emerging sense of oneness with our planet, with each other. (Even in war, today's people sorrowing over human losses also sorrow over the destruction of trees, air, water, animals and plants...)

This book — or better this whole experience of what Matt, Joanna, Veronica, Kevin, Liz and Eddie are all about — seems to me to be a 'backwards and forwards' kind of thing. It will prompt the reader to 'listen to the breathing of the universe' and get away from a way of life that Kevin calls a 'constant throb of noise which dulls the prospect of being surprised'. It will stir the desire to look ahead to what this new unitary stage of consciousness will bring, and with Joanna to feel the presence of the future beings who support our efforts to save the environment for them.

At the same time the voices of Veronica and Elizabeth call us to look backwards to the roots of our existence, to claim and celebrate our traditions, our own aboriginality, to enter into the land and to journey within ourselves to face our darker, shadow side.

Over and over, I found myself dropping my editor's blue pencil to ask myself: what am I — wanderer or urban dweller? black or white? creative dreamer or logical thinker? Or am I all of these? I also found myself returning often to Eddie Kneebone's observation that while we might look up at the sky and talk of stars, planets, and galaxies, the Australian Aboriginals never saw the stars, they only saw their ancestors by the campfires on their journey. *And their eyes met.*

That's the world the book has made me want: the Dreamtime, where everything is now, where I live with my God in the now, at one with all.

As you read, look up from these pages now and then, look sharp, and you may catch the warm eyes returning your gaze from all the campfires of this world.

Catherine Hammond

Creation Spirituality and the Dreamtime

MATTHEW FOX

The beauty that is the Dreamtime is everywhere. The question is: do we have the eyes to see it and the ears to hear it?

I feel it is pure nostalgia to think that only people in the wilderness, in the bush, can experience Dreamtime. It is part of our nature and our histories.

On the other hand, the fact that there is so much wilderness in Australia and that the Australian Aboriginals have lived so long and spent so much spirit in this land does invite people here to a special experience of the wilderness Dreamtime as well. And there is a challenge to bring the two together: how does the outback relate to the urban?

What we need is a *biculturalism*. By this I mean that we need to live both in Dreamtime and in clock time. I am really convinced that we have to find this balance in our civilization. We are so unbalanced. You cannot be a mystic twenty-four hours a day. You would blow all your tubes! You need the dialectic, the dance, the balance.

Is that balance evident in our education system? I know of some cases where it is, some schools that make definite efforts to provide meditation time, gardening time, and art as meditation time for the young. But I don't know of many of this type. In our general education system, it is my experience that in adolescence, at the crucial time of puberty, for example, we take away the crayons, the song and dance, the theatre and we get 'serious'—precisely when we should be bringing the young people more fully into cosmology, introducing them into the Dreamtime of the stars, into the story of the universe.

In fact, this process can begin much sooner now. Some teachers in the United States are giving the creation story to children at a very young age and having them tell the stories about the birth of the stars and the sun. In other words, they are creating rituals with the children.

Ritual is the ultimate way to learn and the implications for growth when these children become teenagers are great. It is creating Dreamtime; the new cosmic story is Dreamtime.

I am convinced that by their nature children live in Dreamtime. Most parents are given children as their spiritual directors. They come as messengers from another place to teach us all the things our parents didn't teach us! Children are mystical beings. But we have to ask: what does our education system do to kill this natural mysticism?

The over-emphasis in our society on comfort makes it difficult for mysticism, for spirituality, to manifest itself. In North America our churches are comfort stations, with padded kneelers, padded seats, air conditioning, the perfect temperature in winter... (I'm told that this is not the case in Australia!). Our attitude toward worship is too comfort-oriented. We need to learn from native peoples in this regard.

One aspect of this comfort orientation regards *time*. We run our worship by the clock, knowing exactly when it will begin, exactly when it will end, and how long it will take to empty the parking lot! Whereas when you worship with native peoples, you find it is a cosmic process. You get in and you wait until everyone is there. At first you're impatient. Most of the time, for most of us, waiting is an uncomfortable thing to do. But then you settle down and begin to realize that waiting is a deep part of the whole spiritual process.

Still on the topic of comfort, a native American sweat lodge is radically uncomfortable. In a sweat lodge you face death. During my first twenty minutes in one, I really thought I was going to die—I was looking for the fire exit! Not finding it, at the end of the twenty minutes, I realized I *was* going to die. It was then that I entered into the consciousness breakthrough that the sweat lodge is all about. I just let go of fear of death and entered into it instead. That's the whole point: real prayer takes one to the brink of things. It takes you to your own transformation.

There's a black American theologian who says he's convinced that ninety-five per cent of all white worship is dead. I asked him, 'How do you define "dead worship"?' His reply was, 'Dead worship is when you walk out the same as when you went in—no transformation took place.'

There *is* a need, therefore, to challenge ourselves, to get out of our comfort orientation. In the Western tradition we confuse asceticism with penance for our sins or hatred of our bodies. But the basic meaning of asceticism relates to being an athlete. An athlete pushes her/himself. There is a point in running or exercising where you go beyond what you thought you could do, where it hurts a little. At this point, ecstacy usually begins. The West moralizes about this process, holding that the hurt is to keep the body down, to punish one's self for being a sexual being, or a sinner... All that has destroyed the real meaning of sacrifice, and of being a spiritual athlete.

An example regarding true asceticism would be to go without water for a couple of days, to go without food for a while, to fast, in other words, but *not* in penance for your sins. Let your sins go! Fast in order to re-experience your own health. The fact is that all religious traditions of any antiquity have fasting periods. Why? Because it is good for our health. Our digestive system is kept working twenty-four hours a day, seven days a week. Give it a break!

We all should fast for that reason alone, a few times a year. This is holism, for in the process of allowing our physical body to be regenerated, our senses do get cleansed, and we do see the world with greater reverence, greater awe, greater gratefulness.

The Western spiritual tradition distorts the whole language of asceticism. Creation mystics are overlooked. We need to redo our theology.

I have been asked what steps should be taken to plant creation spirituality in Australia. I would begin with a seminar exploring creation theology with art-as-meditation gatherings included. And, of course, creating rituals together. Then the follow-up would be very important. Australians must define Australian theology, Australian spirituality, in the light of the creation tradition, and in the light of your Aboriginal roots, as well as the issues of injustice in Australia and your unique experiences of joy and mysticism.

Without doubt, this can be done. Any human group can do it. It is built into us to be able to bring justice about and celebration. That is why we are a gift to the universe and not a curse.

Knowledge of 'the heart' is not alone sufficient. The concepts must be grasped, which requires study. There may be toxic concepts to be undone first of all, for we have been fed dualistic categories through religion, education and culture for centuries. They have to be let go of. We have some cleansing to do of our minds, left brain as well as right brain. The right brain, however, does not need much cleansing; it just needs waking up and exercise.

It is important, then, to gather together in groups; do rituals together; read the mystics together with the right brain, with the heart, putting all this through the body; read our greatest Western mystics — Hildegard and Eckhart, Julian, Mechtid — and don't forget Jesus and the Wisdom literature of the Bible (see the book, *Wisdom's Feast*, by S. Cady, for the latter); study together; apply this to the Australian situation; make contact with Australian Aboriginal people. The latter effort will, of course, be clumsy at first. Why wouldn't it be, with all the pain on both sides?

Victor Lewis, who gives excellent workshops on racism and, as a young black, has been through so much of it, says that white people are in deep grief about racism. Sometimes we hear the anger and suffering from people of colour and we get overwhelmed with guilt. But the real issue is our grief. We have to deal with that sadness.

White Australians have to make themselves vulnerable to the Aboriginal people — whatever that may mean.

Australian Aboriginals must be encouraged to give talks, to go into parishes and speak about their experiences, to make contacts. If Hildegard of Bingen and Meister Eckhart are shared with them, they will become excited!

I'll never forget the first time we translated Hildegard, and I shared her with a class of students. There was a fellow in the class who spoke up after I had read just a few lines. 'I've just returned,' he said, 'from living eighteen years with the Lakota people in South Dakota (native Americans). Hildegard sounds exactly like the medicine man who was my spiritual teacher for the last ten years!' All kinds of energy can flow when native peoples experience the creation tradition.

As Liz Cain has pointed out, spirituality must begin with the land. This is basic to the entire Aboriginal consciousness. It is also basic to the environmental survival not just of our species but of all the species with whom we share this planet. So obviously this whole issue of land — I prefer the word 'wilderness' — is at the heart of things.

It is not easy *growing up, letting go, separating one's self from*... I believe this is the moment in history when Australians are really doing this. You are realizing you are not just transplanted Europeans. We Americans are only beginning to realize that we have to evolve our own theology, not just translate European books and write their footnotes! We have our own experience, *from our own land*! For the land is where the spirits are.

You need to get in touch with your Australian poets, writers and artists both black and white, on this land. They are the ones who are naming the journeys for you. I get very excited when I look back on the writers in my land like Walt Whitman or Annie Dillard, Alice Walker, Ralph Waldo Emerson, Barry Lopez and many others. The spirit of the land is speaking through these people. There is this tradition of creation spirituality in my land. And that is a deep part of my spiritual roots. It will be of yours, too. Find these treasures — the musicians, poets, painters, photographers, novelists and all the writers who can feed your soul *here*, because they have lived here.

There is a special link, I think, between the Australian experience and the North American experience. There is much we hold in common. First of all, I would like to cite a criticism, one that raises our consciousness, from a document in Central America. This document was put together in 1988 by one hundred Christian pastors, lay leaders, and theologians of Central America. It is called the 'Kairos Document', and it images the struggle of the poor there against what it calls 'the idols of the Empire'.

We have the tradition — Australians have it even more than Americans — of piously nodding our heads whenever we hear the word 'empire'. I'll never forget the first time I went into St Paul's Cathedral in London with my eyes open — I was a student at the time. In that Cathedral there are all these huge statues to military men, and underneath them are inscriptions to the effect that so-and-so killed one thousand Indians in such-and-such a battle; and another killed twenty thousand in some other battle. You realize that the marriage of Church and Empire must be critiqued. If we don't do it, someone will do it for us. The Kairos Document is a good example.

The British Empire is admittedly a kind of harmless pussycat at the present time, but the toxin from it is probably still in your consciousness. Today of course what is at issue is the American Empire. And the statement from Central America about this latter empire reads, 'In the process of maturing in their historical consciousness with the help of their faith, Central America's poor came to find out that the God of Western Christian society was not the God of Jesus but rather an idol of the empire.' Now this is strong language. You might substitute the word, 'Australian Aboriginal' for 'Central American'.

'The Central American poor at this time,' continues the document, 'are serving as witnesses and martyrs for the God of Jesus, the God of the poor. They are a living prophecy that invites the Christian Churches to abandon the empire's gods and become converted to the true God.' Again, that is strong language. I think we have to wrestle with it, put it into our prayer and our discussions. But it's very traditional language, it's Biblical. The idols of the empire are false gods — imperialism, colonialism, slavery, racism, sexism — false gods that must be dealt with — openly.

Barry Lopez' book, *Of Wolves and Men*, really moves me and I have quoted from it in my writing. Here is a man who went to live with wolves in Canada for a whole year or two. He *lived with them* and then wrote this marvellous book, which is a wonderful cleansing of our soul. We have a lot of mythology about how evil wolves are and how they are out to get us. There is a projection of the 'bogyman' onto wolves. Lopez brings out the beauty of the wolf, as well of course as the terror that is intrinsically associated with all wild animals (including the human! — just look at our history . . .).

Father Bartholomew de las Casas was a Dominician priest who strongly defended the Indians in Latin America against the Spanish. He underwent a conversion, for he himself was Spanish. In fighting very hard for the rights of the Indians, he made the point: that an excuse used by the Spanish to justify their killing the Indians was that the latter practiced human sacrifice. This was true: part of their ritual was to sacrifice a young man or woman once a year or thereabouts. But, argued Bartholomew, all the sacrifices that the Indians performed as ritual over the years do not come close to the number of killings for which the Spanish are responsible. He further declared that the Indian civilization was superior to the Spanish.

De las Casas' final point was that if, in the history of the world, there has ever been cause for a just war, 'these native people have the right to make war against the white Europeans until Judgment Day'.

Columbus landed in America in 1492. We are quite close to the commemoration of that event. I purposely do not use the word 'celebration'. There will be a lot of people celebrating it, but that is not how the Indians see it. Five hundred years ago, when Columbus landed, there were eighty million native people in America. Fifty years later, there were only ten million! Seventy million native people died after the Europeans landed —some by disease, yes, but a great many by genocide.

I have read statistics about Australia and New Zealand, and it must be admitted that this same story is repeated everywhere. It is time now for acknowledgment and grief.

There is a fine book on this topic by Frederick Turner called, *Beyond Geography*. It is a history of America from the point of view of the native people, beginning with Columbus. Turner calls it an essay in spirituality, in the history of spirituality, for he feels that the reason, the *fundamental* reason for the genocide was European spirituality.

It is his belief that Europeans had repressed the sensual, the sexual, and the darker side; so when they came to America, all this surfaced and was projected onto the native peoples whom they called 'savages'. The killing of this 'enemy' (which was really themselves) was thus justified and legitimized.

I am always asking: what does a homophobic society lose in its soul when it offends a sexual minority? Likewise, what has white Christianity lost in its soul in lashing out at other civilizations? This is not an altruistic question. It is a matter of self-interest: what have we lost in our souls?

In listening to what Australian Aboriginals have to say to us, I experience a sense of complimentarity. The gifts of Christianity do bring something to the native people of Australia, and the gifts of the Aboriginals do give something to Christianity. This is the challenge: to work out that complementarity.

I am convinced that one sign of hope for the world of today is that the wisdom of the native peoples is still around. But it won't be for long unless we change our white ways.

In one of his essays, *The Passing Wisdom of Birds*, Barry Lopez has a wonderful passage with an incredible message. It relates to the conquest by Cortez of what is now Mexico City. That city was the Aztec Byzantium. Everyone, including Cortez himself, considered it the most beautiful city in the world. Among its delights were aviaries of marvellous, multi-colored birds. Nearly every home had its own aviary. Now Cortez was driven out when he first entered the city, so two years later, he returned with his army and destroyed the entire city — including all the aviaries. He wiped out even the birds!

I want to share with you Barry Lopez' thoughts in this context because I really feel they speak to the issue of the land, of the wilderness, and of our attitudes toward it. Lopez tells us that when we lose even the birds, we face losing the purpose of our ideals, our sense of dignity and compassion — even our sense of what we call God. He believes that eight thousand years ago, in the Fertile Crescent, we set aside the Mother Goddess tradition but we can locate it again and creatively refine it in North America. The same could be said of Australia.

For Barry Lopez, the new world is still resonant with mystery. In this context I have goose bumps at the thought of the parts of Australia I have seen, especially the central part. I feel the truth of Barry's words for Australia. He calls for an enlightened reponse toward cultures that differ from our own, and by culture he does not mean just the human. He is also talking about wolves, birds, invertebrates... Barry believes that we can find the sense of resolution we have been seeking for centuries by moving away from the traditional narrow view of the value of life and beginning to respect other paths to perfection.

I find this to be an incredible outlook and I lay it before you. Eight thousand years ago our species took a turn away from nature, and God in nature. Now the reality is that you Australians are being invited — through the mystery still in your land, the spirits still on your land, and the Australian Aboriginal peoples not only outside you but *in* you, as well as your Celtic ancestors — to take another look and recover even the meaning of God.

Let me turn now to the very rich topic of the Dreamtime. When new thoughts are first encountered, they are not always grasped immediately. So it was for me regarding the incredibly rich concept of the Dreamtime. I first read about it a few years ago, but it is only now just beginning to seep into me. There is such wisdom in this whole Dreamtime concept.

Let me begin by pointing out the connections between our biblical heritage, mysticism and the Dreamtime. Elizabeth Cain has called our attention to the fact that there is no word for *time* in the Australian Aboriginal language. Everything is always *now*. This is exactly how Meister Eckhart talks. 'God,' says he, 'is always in the beginning, making things new!' And he adds, 'If you can return to the beginning, you will always be new, always be young, always be in touch with God.' This is why our Scriptures begin with 'In the beginning . . .'—both Genesis and John's Gospel. And all four Gospels begin with the creation story, a cosmic creation story, as I have demonstrated in my book, *The Coming of the Cosmic Christ*. The cosmic Christ is celebrated in the first chapters of each of the Synoptic Gospels, just as he is in the first chapter of John's Gospel.

Another phrase Eckhart uses is 'living in the eternal now'. What we find in the Australian Aboriginal understanding of time is a hundred per cent pure mystical consciousness. We white people will never get it until we sink into our own mystical experience. That explains the clash between white and indigenous cultures.

We have to listen with our hearts, not just our heads, as Eckhart says, 'God is creating the entire universe, fully and totally, in this present *now*'.

'*This* is the Dreamtime,' Eddie Kneebone says, '*now*'. Eddie would undoubtedly feel that Meister Eckhart is an Australian Aboriginal too!

All the stories of original creation are Dreamtime. It is all *now*. This view is, of course, scientifically correct. All nineteen billion years of history are behind us. They don't exist any more. The original fireball is gone. The supernova explosion that gave birth to the elements of our body is gone. But it is present in today's sunshine, in today's photosynthesis, in *our* bodies and minds.

Every time an idea 'goes off' in our brains, we make a connection. A light wave goes off, a photon; that light wave is a piece of the sun, and the sun is a piece of a supernova explosion which in turn was a piece of the original fireball. *The fireball is going off in your brain now*, because everything that happened up to now doesn't exist any more. There is no yesterday. It's like a wave coming up in the ocean — it brings everything with it.

What Eckhart is saying is verifiable by today's physics, *which is mystical*, and it's verifiable by the Australian Aboriginal tradition, *which is mystical*. (It is not, however, very verifiable in most church rituals or church thinking as yet... But you and I are going to make that happen — in politics and education too.)

There is definitely much in common between Eckhart's spirituality and that of the Australian Aboriginal. The reason, I believe, is that Eckhart lived with the Celtic spirit in the Rhineland. Indeed, I would say that we have an Eckhart only because the Celts settled in the Rhineland. That settlement is behind what is called the Rhineland mystic movement. This fact, too, explains the emergence of a Hildegard of Bingen. Hildegard attended a Celtic monastery which was, by way of interest, a monastery of both sexes.

Unlike the Jansenist Irish, the Celts were not all hung up on sex, and they had men and women residing in monasteries together, thus benefiting from their common energy.

Again, another interesting fact here is that Hildegard had to break away because the men became very jealous of the great fame she achieved as a result of the books she wrote. Many women wanted to study with Hildegard in the monastery, but the men would not make room for them, even though they could easily have done so.

'Enough of this injustice!' cried Hildegard, and she left — taking with her not only her own dowry but also those of all the other women with her! For years the abbot wrote her poison-pen letters demanding that she come back — and to be sure to bring the dowries back with her. Hildegard never returned. Instead, she started three women's monasteries. When she did reply to the abbot, her letter was all about injustice. That was the incomparable Hildegard.

So, in the Celtic Rhineland mystical tradition, Meister

Eckhart could write, 'God is creating the entire universe, fully and totally, in this present *now*. Everything that God created six thousand years ago (according to the science of his day) and even previous to that ... God creates now *all at once.*' He goes on to collapse future and past into now: 'Everything of the past and everything of the present and everything of the future God is creating in the innermost realms of the soul.' This is good Australian Aboriginal thinking. And it is good physics, too, because it is true.

What we give birth to is the future. If we continue on our way of destroying the wilderness, destroying the habitat, that comes out of the present. But if there is something churning in our hearts and souls now, in the innermost depths of our psyches, to redirect our species, then that is how the future will look.

What emphasis all this puts on creativity, on the choices we make with our divine powers of imagination! I cannot listen to Australian Aboriginals speaking for very long without hearing the echo from their heart about the fact that everything is happening *now*.

Dreamtime itself is right here now. When, as a Christian theologian, I hear the word 'Dreamtime', I hear Jesus talking about the Kingdom of God. 'The kingdom and queendom of God, the reign of God, is here.' We are in it.

In his explanation of Dreamtime, Eddie Kneebone makes it clear that all living things are part of it, including the souls and spirits of the ancestors that are in the trees, in the animals. Is not this the Christian doctrine of the Communion of the Saints? This Communion of Saints is *here, now*. Hildegard is sitting on your shoulder, urging you to be as stubborn as she was in her time, and as creative. Eckhart, too, and all the saints are here.

During my last sabbatical, I did a Vision Quest, which is a native American ritual. You go out into the woods for twenty-four hours, fasting beforehand, and you pray. It was a very powerful experience for me. One thing I learned from it is that the native American people believe God does not make evil

spirits; we humans do, and our human institutions do. Moreover, the only avenue by which an evil spirit can enter the
human heart is *fear*. That is their belief. Fear is the doorway
through which evil spirits of others or of institutions enter our
hearts. And prayer is geared to making ourselves strong enough
to resist that fear, or to enter into it without succumbing to it.

What amazing wisdom is embodied in this belief! — evil
spirits come from humans, from institutions, and fear is the
avenue of entrance.

Fundamentalism, which is spreading through all religions —
Islam, Judaism, Buddhism, and certainly Christianity — is all
about fear. Courage is at the heart of fighting the fear.

Another thing I learned at the Vision Quest was about the
spirits of the place. All the leaves came alive during that
twenty-four hours, with images of animals. The whole forest
was illuminated for the twenty-four hours. There was even a
madonna up in the tree. When my director for the Quest, Buck
Ghosthorse, processed it with me afterwards, he said; 'You
know, these spirits are the spirits of all the animals who have
lived in this land.'

We're talking here about dinosaurs, crocodiles, polar bears
... But the point he was making was that the spirits are
present, and they are supportive. They want to see creative
spirituality happen and expand with the human species, because
it is to their advantage.

The Communion of Saints is on our side, but it does not
involve just the two-legged ones. Thomas Merton — who has a
half claim on being from Down Under, since his father was a
New Zealander — says that every non-two-legged creature is a
saint! (Something to remember when we're about to swat a
mosquito?! During the Vision Quest we were forbidden to kill
any mosquitoes. At one time, I had thirty on me, and that
proved interesting...)

The Communion of Saints, thus, takes in all creatures, and
they all have soul. Our ancestors believed that. Only in the
eighteenth century, with the Enlightenment and Descartes,
came the idea that humans alone have souls. Descartes held

that if a dog were cut and it squealed, this would be a mechanical response only. That was the beginning of Behaviourism — and our Western medicine, too. But Aquinas in the Middle Ages taught that animals and plants have souls.

I'd go even further. I think rocks and mountains have their own sense of soul too — they just act a little slower... Today's physics tells us that every rock is a cyclone of activity. The atoms in the rock are jumping around. Indeed everything is moving in the universe, everything is dancing the cosmic dance... except a few white Christians... in high places...

I am connecting the tradition of the Kingdom of God to Dreamtime, and the tradition of the Communion of Saints to Dreamtime. Here is material for Australian theologians to work on. Eddie Kneebone declared that what Dreamtime gives people is a powerful identity, a sense of their importance, a belief that they are valuable for what they are.

Another aspect of the Dreamtime is *cosmology*. It is a realization that we have a place in the universe. *Our lives are not trivial!* The young need to hear this. The Australian Aboriginal young people feel so dispossessed precisely because that message has been ripped away. Yet it was part of the Original Blessing, part of the cosmic gift.

At this point, I'd like to mention something Eddie Kneebone alluded to: the Australian Aboriginal feeling about the views of anthropologists. I resonate to this because the native people in America have the same feeling toward anthropologists. They're being told something similar to what Eddie spoke of: that their ancestors originally came from Europe, walked over the Bering Strait and settled in North America. About ten years ago, anthropologists were saying that the Indians may have been in North America only about six to eight thousand years. Later they said the figure could be twelve thousand. But two years ago, in Florida, they found a sweat lodge, upside down, and they carbon-dated it back forty-two thousand years!

Buck Ghosthorse, the Lakota Native American whom I mentioned above, comments, 'Oh, we've no problem with the theory that these folks came over the Bering Strait. The point is that when they arrived, we shook their hands and welcomed them!'

Buck also used to quote his grandfather as saying, 'Don't worry about these white people. They're just passing through!'

Another Indian has remarked, 'Sometimes I just sit myself down next to a freeway and I watch all these white people going places all the time, just going and going — they're never *there!*' Yet part of the Kingdom of God motif of the Dreamtime is that we *are* there! That is what Jesus is trying to tell us: the Kingdom is already here, it *is* among us! This is called in the Western theological tradition 'realized eschatology'.

We put so much energy into getting away from wherever we are, instead of putting the same energy into preparing our hearts to see the wonder that is already here with us, where we are. Doing the latter is what is meant by simplifying our lifestyle.

If the Australian Aboriginals could be happy for thousands of years in the desert, with none of the so-called comforts of life, they must have something going for them. And that *something* is a whole sense of *being there*.

These, then, are some reflections I wanted to offer in the light of our own Western tradition. Perhaps this is the time for us who are ex-Europeans to start cleaning up the mess left by Western spirituality, in the name of empire, around the world. We may need to do some meditating on how best to do that, and how to ritualize it. What has to be realized is that we have inherited a dysfunctional spirituality from the recent centuries of Christianity.

The deeper roots of our Catholic tradition, however, tell a different story. Let us recall that it was the Irish, the Celts of the twelfth century, who re-Christianized Europe, brought it to life, made it creation-centred, and gave us our wonderful mystical traditions, from Francis of Assisi to Hildegard of Bingen.

In Northern Italy alone there are over two hundred churches

dedicated to Francis. The Celts were responsible for that! Francis is deeply Celtic in his spirituality. But we need to rescue Francis from being sentimentalized! (In the States, popular custom places him in backyard birdbaths!)

Sentimentality is not spirituality. It is spirituality's Number One Enemy. Carl Jung makes the point that sentimentalism and violence always go together: scratch a sentimentalist and you find violence. The issues related to violence, such as racism and injustice, are never dealt with in the sentimental context. Justice is not a category of sentimentalism. Syrupy emotion has nothing to do with a real passion for justice. But the Celts had an authentic spirituality.

Thus we can affirm that the healthy intellectual history of Europe was led by the Celts. It was they who first translated the Eastern theologians for the Latin West. In fact, with regard to Thomas Aquinas, there is an interesting and not well known fact that bears this out.

When Thomas was about seventeen, a student at the University of Naples, his main teacher was a Celt, an Irishman, and this man was teaching Aristotle to him—a very radical thing to be doing in those days! For Aristotle was a pagan scientist, and the Augustinian theologians who were the fundamentalists and sentimentalists of the thirteenth century—the people representing the establishment, the 'empire' that Augustine had set up in the fourth century—these men were horrified at the thought of bringing in a cosmology from a pagan scientist like Aristotle. Moreover, the Pope had actually forbidden Christians to read Aristotle (and Naples is not very far from Rome . . .!).

Notwithstanding all this, Aquinas' Irish scholar was teaching him Aristotle, and Aquinas was to spend his whole life bringing Aristotle—the best scientist they could find in the thirteenth century—into the heart of Christianity. And with him, cosmology.

I am presently doing work on Aquinas' mysticism. We were always told that he was a rationalist, but he was not. His best mystical works have hardly ever been translated into English: his biblical commentaries and his commentary on Pseudo Denys.

All the Thomists through the centuries have come and gone, without bothering to translate the commentaries. Yet these commentaries are the least scholastic and the most cosmological. I have found some really wonderful things in these books!

Coming again to the Dreamtime category, I want to repeat that I find it immensely rich. It is all about the ongoing creation story. And it's about mysticism, the eternal *now*, that to which Jesus called us: the awareness of the kingdom and queendom of God being here. From this consciousness comes compassion. People realize that where there is unnecessary suffering, where there is injustice, there is no kingdom and queendom of God. It is about opening our hearts to the *joy* of the present moment — that is, realized eschatology.

In conclusion, I am convinced that here in Australia you are living a unique theological moment. This is the time to delve into the deep meaning of Dreamtime. The only way to do it is through your own mystical tradition, which needs to be plummeted. It cannot be understood any other way.

Waking Up in the Turning Time

JOANNA MACY

This last decade of the millennium is a turning time for us, a turning time for our planet. I want to reflect with you about what it is like for us to be alive in this time — not only to hear its summons, to see the promise, but to be fully present to what is happening to our world *now*.

Along with 'liberation', Matthew Fox often uses the word 'awakening'. *Waking up* is what the Buddha did. He *woke up*. The name of the Sarrodaya movement that I worked with in Sri Lanka, a Buddhist self-help movement that has been active in over five thousand villages, means 'waking up together'. This is what we too are challenged to do: wake up together.

We have seen some pretty exciting 'waking up' recently. In December, 1989, on my way back from India to my home in California, I stopped in Germany. Everyone could talk of nothing else but the excitement of what was happening. 'The walls are coming down! The inner walls, the outer walls!' I was moved and enlightened to hear from my friends and acquaintances how this extraordinary *turning* in Eastern Europe, this rejection of forty years of totalitarian regimes in such a quick and mostly bloodless way, had as a key emphasis the destruction of the environment.

In country after country, city after city, where this great turning came, it was love for the environment and determination to prevent its destruction that was rallying people as much as demand for political freedom. In Hungary, where I had been doing some ecology workshops a few months before, I was told that the people's very first display of autonomous will was a silent march through the streets of Budapest to protest a massive hydroelectric project. Sponsored by the Austrian, Czech and Hungarian governments, this project threatened to destroy the Danube. It was that threat to their natural world, their entire regional ecosystem, that brought them out on the streets.

In East Germany, at those extraordinary Monday night meetings in the churches in Leipzig that led to the overthrow of the government, political freedom was not the only rallying cry. The people were also impelled by profound environmental concerns — the poisoning of their rivers, the deforestation, the turning of that once beautiful land into a moonscape.

At the Berlin wall, as the people were pouring through for the first time, an East German was asked, 'Well, are you going to move to West Germany now?' His reply was, 'No way! I'm going to stay right here and clean up, and in ten years you're going to be pouring through here to *our* beautiful ecological republic!'

Knowing where home is, knowing that it can be cleaned up, knowing that we can do it — it is to this that we are called. And the excitement that we all felt as we watched those events in Eastern Europe was not because they were choosing a consumerist society — God help us! — nor because we saw the change as a triumph of capitalism, but perhaps because we saw in it a promise: our brothers and sisters were awakening, as we can awaken too — to heal our common home.

Waking up together. Recently, at the Smithsonian Institute in Washington, a conference was held on global environmental problems. Scientists met to try to puzzle out why the very clear warning signals, universally recognized and widely publicized, are not being followed by action. They pointed out that global environmental deterioration is more deeply threatening than most people think. It is going to be more difficult to ameliorate than most people think. And it is coming at us much faster than most people think.[1] They were perplexed to see that their warnings and the mounting evidence supporting them have produced few changes in government policies or personal lifestyles.

What will it take for us to make the changes that technologically are within our reach? The Smithsonian conference suggested that our society is still in denial.

Great inner and collective truth work needs to be done. I use 'truth work' in the sense that Gandhi used the phrase, satyagraha —'truth power', the power of speaking the truth.

It was wonderful to begin the decade of the nineties hearing a new chief of state speak the truth! I am referring to the words of President Vaclav Havel of Czechoslovakia. He said: 'For forty years you have heard on this day from the mouths of my predecessors the same thing—"our country is flourishing", "we believe in our government and beautiful prospects are open to us". I assume that you have not named me to this office so that I too should lie to you. Our country is *not* flourishing. The great creative and spiritual potential of our nation is *not* being applied meaningfully. Entire branches of industry are producing things for which there is no demand.'

I consider Havel's to be one of the great speeches of all time, an honour to this playwright-become-president. He can teach us how to talk straight, to speak our dreams, yes, but also to call it the way it is. This is an essential part of the healing, an essential part of the awakening.

Havel went on: 'The state which calls itself a state of workers is humiliating and exploiting them. Our outmoded economy wastes energy... We've spoiled our land, rivers and forests inherited from our ancestors [Oh my, if we could only hear an American president saying something like that!] and we have today the worst environment in the whole of Europe... The worst of it is that we live in a spoiled moral environment. We have become morally ill because we are used to saying one thing and thinking another.

'Out of talented and responsible people ingeniously husbanding their land, our government has made cogs of some sort of great, monstrous, thudding, smelly machine with an unclear purpose. All it can do is slowly, irresistibly, wear itself out, with all its cogs.

'If I speak about our spoiled moral atmosphere, I am not referring only to our masters... I'm speaking about all of us. For all of us have grown used to the totalitarian system and accepted it as an immutable fact, thereby actually helping to keep it going. None of us is only its victims; we are all also responsible for it. We can't blame it on something foreign, on something inherited from a distant relative. On the contrary, we must accept this heritage as something we have inflicted on ourselves. If we accept it in such a way, we shall come to understand that it is up to all of us to do something about it.'

What will it take for us to begin to experience the invigo-rating, clarifying pull of that kind of truth, of that crystalline kind of vision that will help us wake up?

Moreover, to what dimensions can we wake up at this time? We can awaken to our pain, to our love for our world, to time, to the reinhabitation of deep time, and lastly, to our larger self—what and who we really are.

My brothers and sisters, we share the same planet. In your faces, I see the faces of brothers and sisters who inhabit the other side of the globe from where I live, but it's the same globe. The circulation of poisons through our seas, the dumping of radioactive wastes and the decimation of our soils and forest lands—these things know no national boundaries. They are not limited to one segment of our planet.

We are all inhabiting this planet at the same moment in time. It is our fate, our karma, our extraordinary privilege and terror to be alive at this time when our planet could die as a home for conscious life. I'm not telling you anything you don't know.

We must wake up to what's happening to our world, to the very air we breathe and the water we drink, to our fellow species, to the very basis of our life.

A lot of my time is spent working with people around the world about how we deal with our inner responses to the plight of our planet, because I believe that if we were really convinced, we'd know what to do. This dying off, this sickening of our world, this exploitation is not visited on us by some extraterrestrial force or some satanic deity. It is the product of *our* actions and *our* lifestyles and *our* decisions. If we acknowledge the crisis situation, action will follow—just as we rush forward to pull a child from beneath the wheels of a truck.

So it is that befriending our pain, living with and learning from our own inner responses to what is happening to our world are key factors in our *waking up*. This is critical because we live in a culture that is afraid of hardship and pain. Fear of pain keeps us from being able to hear the painful news. It keeps us stuck because we are always stuck with what we don't let ourselves experience. The minute we befriend that normal, wholesome grief for our world, acknowledging it, it will flow. We will realize that this grief comes from caring, and the caring from our deep inter-connectedness, and we will be freed to act.

Barbara Mor, ecofeminist and author of *The Great Cosmic Mother: Rediscovering the Religion of the Earth*, has this to say: 'In this post-everything real decade (post–politics, post–feminism, post–consciousness) there's a corresponding decadent compunction to Look Good: spiritually, physically, culturally: pose pretty. Appear-to-have-it-all-together. As a substitute for real substance, genuine power. Even our goddesses. New Age, spiritual guides, even we spiritual feminists, urge ourselves to image "positively": smiling, wise, benevolent, graciously non-confrontational ladies. Those who succor, shelter, soothe, agree and understand. Goddesses of therapy rather than bitches of politics; goddesses of personal wellbeing rather than witches of global change. Healing, not upheaval, because we are all, as the whole doomed world is, alone, scared, in pain, stressed-out, terminally obstructed, overdosed and confused.

'Naturally it follows that we seek the Mother of Peace and Quiet, not an Amazonian Battle-Axe hounding us out to Fight Again. In the midst of patriarchy's metallic noise and violent self-pollution, we consume tapes of our mother's last, lost waterfalls, forest winds, sweet silence. For our Goddess we prefer the lovely and aerobic nurturer, Ms Wholistic Healing Sunshine . . .'[2]

I find in those words what was outstanding in President Havel's speech: the same healthy, invigorating willingness to acknowledge what isn't pretty.

So in this turning time we need to stop anesthetizing ourselves, to stop reaching for the pain killers. It's the time for saying: yes, we know how to suffer with our world. Once we're ready to do that, we find out who we are.

Another spiritual trap that I encounter is the belief that suffering somehow reveals a personal flaw or mistake. Any pain we may experience in beholding our world derives from our own attachments, which we should — if we're 'spiritual' enough — let go of, or transcend. In this view suffering itself is seen as dysfunctional, revealing some neurotic maladjustment. But the truth is that if we are *not* able to suffer with what is happening in our world, *that* is a real illness. When we own our pain for the world, we wake up to our living connections with it.

This coming alive can be painful, just as it hurts when the blood begins to circulate through a limb that has been asleep. Yet in the discomfort, in the grief and the rage at the wrecking of our world, there is profound health.

Still another spiritual trap that I encounter is the belief that the world is already perfect. One therefore meditates on this perfection and feels so peaceful that the world itself will become peaceful without the need for action . . .

All of these views are variations, I think, of something we've inherited from the last 2000 years of patriarchy. That 'something' is the fear and loathing of matter. It is time now to outgrow that outlook and, as Matthew Fox so beautifully invites us to do, enter into the mystery of flesh and tree and rock. It is time to experience the awe and beauty of what we can call deep materialism.

As we wake up to our pain, we wake up to our love for the world, because they are two sides of the same coin. That's why so many of us are afraid to love — it invites pain.

In the great religious traditions, the relationship to our world has been imaged in a number of ways. I shall describe four of them. One is to view the world as a battleground; another to view the world as a trap; the other two, which appeal to me more, are to view the world as a lover and to view it as self. Each of these possibilities appears in each of the great religious traditions.

The World As A Battleground. Here good and evil are pitted against each other, the forces of light battle the forces of darkness. We see this view at work in the growth of fundamentalism, which is to be found in every tradition. It goes way back through history and appeals to our hunger for security, to our need to believe that we are on the side of the angels. But we don't have time to indulge in that sort of fantasy any more.

Nor can we afford the second view: *The World As A Trap.* Here the spiritual journey is seen as the effort to extricate oneself from the toils of matter, so as to move upward toward ever purer realms of mind and light. The journey up out of matter, which the heroic ego is called to achieve, breeds an ambivalent love/hate relationship with the very element on which we are dependent. The material world is seen as something to be conquered either by accumulating or by wiping it out.

In sharp contrast, there are those who are ready to have a Love Affair with their world. And that is the third view: *World As Lover.* Recently I came across the words of someone who learned to love his world as I believe we are meant to. Thomas Traherne, a seventeenth century English cleric, tells us: 'Your enjoyment of the world is never right till you so esteem it that everything in it is more your treasure than a king's exchequer full of gold and silver... Your enjoyment of the world is never right till every morning you awake in heaven, see yourself in your Father's palace and look upon the skies and the earth and the air as celestial joys... The bride of a monarch in her husband's chamber has no such causes of delight as you...

'You never enjoy the world aright until the sea itself floweth in your veins, till you're clothed with the heavens and crowned with the stars and perceive yourself to be the sole heir of the whole world, and more than so because people are in it who are every one sole heirs as well as you.

'Till your spirit filleth the whole world and stars are your jewels; till you are as familiar with the work of God in all ages as with your walk and table . . . you never enjoy the world. Till you feel it more than your private estate and are more present in the hemisphere; considering the glories and the beauties there, than in your own house; till you remember how lately you were made and how wonderful it was when you came into it . . .

'You never enjoy the world aright till you so live the beauty of enjoying it that you are earnest to persuade others to enjoy it, and so perfectly hate the abominable corruption of men in despising it that you would rather suffer the flames of hell than willingly be guilty of their error. There is so much blindness and ingratitude and damned folly in it. The world is a mirror of infinite beauty, yet no man sees it.'[3]

The fourth view of which I spoke is very close to this and can also be found in all the great religious traditions. We can wake up to our world as to *Our Larger Self*. We can move out of the mistaken notion that we are separate, isolated and competitive beings. We can shift aside from our conventional identification, stretching that metaphorical piece of turf that we call the self and around which we construct our strategies and our self-interest. We can come to know our true identity as our planet, an identity interexistent with all beings.

This perspective allows us to expand vastly our experience of time. And the need for us to do that is great. For one of the most extraordinary phenomena of our epoch is the way we are squeezing ourselves into a tight, tiny compartment of time, in which we hurry ever more frenetically.

Studies on our contemporary experience of time show us to be inhabiting an ever shrinking span.

We are losing touch with our past and disregarding our future. Psychologically and spiritually disconnected from those who for eons loved and tended the land and from those who will inherit it, we pillage our planet.

Now in the closing decade of our millennium, there is an urgent need for us to reconnect with past and future. We need to reinhabit time. The gifts for us in doing so are enormous. I want to mention two.

First of all, by liberating ourselves from the little squirrel cage we live in, by reinhabiting time, we have our true lifespan restored to us. We were not born yesterday. Every atom in our body goes back to the dawn of space and time. In the deep ecology work that I and my colleagues have been doing around the world, we practice remembering our evolutionary journey. This journey is coded in us, in our very cells and neural system. There is knowledge in our bodies of phylogenetic sequences through time, and we can tap it through the power of our intention and imagination. The human chapter that we're presently living is just the last few seconds of the planet-day that we have lived. Through this kind of 'remembering' we can alter our sense of lifespan. We can see and experience ourselves as coterminous with our planet.

All this is a marvellous source for the courage that it takes to do what must be done. When we stand up to our governments and our corporations, when we engage in direct action, when we lobby, when we organize in our communities, it is not out of some personal whim or even personal virtue. Rather, we stand and we move with the full authority of our four-and-a-half-billion-year life! It is the life, that has brought us here through all the eons, that can sing us through these final years of the second millennium, into the turning we need to make. We have reserves of courage and reserves of ingenuity with which we were gifted by our fish ancestors, by our primate ancestors, by rock and storm and volcano, by our planet. The song of life is unfolding through us. This, then, is one gift of the reinhabitation of time.

Another gift is partnership with beings of the future. This is an experience to which I was led through my work with the issue of radioactive wastes. We are challenged here by substances we produce which can cripple and maim and kill for over a quarter of a million years. Confronting the enormity of this problem, I knew that no matter what else we create it will be what we do with these voluminous and deadly wastes that will matter most of all to the beings of the future. So I asked them for their guidance in helping develop ways of guarding these wastes, and I asked them for the sense of their presence. Over the years they've become—I hope I don't sound too crazy!—quite real for me. They've become so real in fact that I feel sometimes they're right behind my shoulder, and if I were to turn real quick, I might even see them...

I think our sense of separation from them is a function of how our consciousness handles time. As an analogy, think of the way a narrow beam of light would move around a dark room and light up first a chair, then a bookcase, then a piano, then a lamp—we'd see each piece of furniture in a sequential fashion, but if we turned the lights on, it would all be there present at once. Putting this into different spiritual belief systems, we might speak of a blink of the eye of God or a day in the life of Brahma, but the point is that we co-exist with our fellow beings of the past and the future. I believe that they have a stake in what we do now, in *this* time and that we must not feel lonely. We must not feel benighted because of the fact that we are living in such a dangerous and frightening time. Rather we should feel the companionship and encouragement of all our fellow beings.

I'm inspired by the work of a wonderful friend, a Vietnamese Buddhist teacher and monk. His name is Thich Nhat Hanh and he taught here in Australia. An Australian film was made about him, called *The Awakening Bell*. I would like to quote from one of his poems, which I consider a love poem. Let us listen to its message of love coming to us from this Buddhist monk.

'Being rock, Being gas, Being mist, Being mind,
Being the mesons travelling among galaxies with the speed of light,
You have come here, my beloved one.
Your eyes shine so beautiful and deep

You've taken the path traced for you by both the
non-beginning and the never-ending.
On your way here you have gone through millions of births
and deaths.
Innumerable times you have been transformed into
firestorms in outer space.
You have used your own body to measure the age of the
mountains and rivers.
You have manifested yourself as trees, as grass, as
butterflies, as single-celled beings and as
chrysanthemums...
Your smile now invites me into the game whose beginning
no-one knows, The game of hide and seek.'

The end of this poem refers to a *waking up* in our time. What it
suggests is that not just one Buddha is going to wake up. There
is a reference to the Udumbara flower, which in Buddhist
mythology, blooms whenever a Buddha is about to be born. But
there's a difference this time. This time there is a waking up
together. Here is the ending:

'The great Mendicant of old is still there,
on the vulture peak,
contemplating the ever-splendid sunset.
Gotama! How strange!
Who said that the Udumbara flower blooms only once every
five thousand years?
That sound of rising tide —
You can't help hearing it if you have an attentive ear.'[4]
      Thich Nhat Hanh 'The Old Mendicant', Parallax Press

You can't help knowing then that this time it's all of us who
have to wake up together. That is the rising tide.
Something in us wants to be born. It wants to move out from
a centuries-long, millennia-long misidentification in this separate self. This movement is to be found in all the religious
traditions.

To close, I draw from D. H. Lawrence a description of what it is like to *wake up*:

> 'When we get out of the glass bottles of our ego
> and when we escape
> like squirrels turning in the cage of our personality
> and get into the forest again, we shall shiver
> with cold and fright.
> But things will happen to us
> so that we don't know ourselves.
> Cool, unlying life will rush in,
> and passion will make our
> bodies taut with power.
> We shall stamp our feet with new power
> and old things will fall down.
> We shall laugh, and
> institutions will curl up
> like burnt paper.'[5]

NOTES
1. Holden, Prof. J., *Los Angeles Times*, Sept 17, 1989, p 4.
2. Sjoo, Monica and Barbara Mor, *The Great Cosmic Mother: Rediscovering the Religion of the Earth*, Harper San Francisco, 1987.
3. Traherne, T., *Centuries of Meditation*, Faith Press, London; Harper Collins, N.Y., N.Y., 1960.
4. Hanh, Thich Nhat, *The Old Mendicant*, Parallax Press, Berkeley, California.
5. Lawrence, D. H., "*Escape*", *Complete Poems of D. H. Lawrence*, ed. Vivian de Sola and Warren Roberts, vols. 1, 2, Heinemann, London, 1964.

Called By the Land to Enter the Land

VERONICA BRADY

There is, I think, a more than usual significance in this title, not only in the double meaning of the word 'land' which it implies but also, and especially, in the initial word, 'called'. That in itself is a kind of profession of faith. The universe, it suggests, is not one-dimensional but dialogical. There is for each of us and for each creature a particular call, a part to weave in the cosmic dance, a self to fulfil and to be. Here, now, in this place, at this time, we are called to listen, to be attentive, to obey our call (the word obedience has as its root meaning the verb 'to hear').

But it is important to insist also on its particularity. The call comes to each of us individually but also and crucially as part of a community which belongs — since we are concerned with our being-in-our-bodies as our being-in-the-world — in a particular place at a particular moment of history. So the call comes to us as non-Aboriginal Australians, not as Americans on the one hand nor as Aboriginals on the other. We are who we are and are called as and who we are.

We had a parable given us recently — a sign, if you like — of the continuing giftedness of existence. One of our Australian Aboriginal friends at the Creation Spirituality Conference found himself locked out of his room. There was nobody around with a master key and we were all asleep in our own rooms. Indeed, none of us could have let him into his room because none of us had a master key. So he had to get himself in. He tried climbing, standing on a rubbish bin to get a start. He fell several times into the bushes, which broke his fall. None of us heard that though—we were soundly asleep. Finally, he got in, dragging himself through his window and settled down in the building with the rest of us.

Is the point of the parable that maybe we need not sleep soundly? Or is it that we are locked too tightly into our own rooms and do not realize with whom we are sharing the house of creation, or of our part of it? Or is it that we should have shared a room with him? Whatever it might be, I suggest that it makes an essential point, namely that we are not Australian Aboriginals and that, for the time being at least, we live in a different room and must come to terms with who we are there.

To think otherwise, to pretend that we are 'Aboriginals in spirit' may be both delusive and dangerous, a form of sentimentality, a 'working off in words of feelings we haven't really got', to use D. H. Lawrence's definition. They are the ancient people of the land who have lived here for at least 40,000 years. At the very most, we have been here a mere 202 years.

Who, then, are we?

We non-Aboriginal Australians are all more or less recent migrants, people called—or pushed—out of our own lands to this country on the other side of the world. Very few of us have come from this side of the Equator; the Pacific peoples and the South Americans are the only ones to do so. We have come, that is, to our Antipodes, to a land very different from our own. To a greater or lesser extent, we are displaced people.

Anna Couani, a recent migrant, once put it: 'My family comes from two different countries and lives in a third country. We gave away the idea of "home". We laugh at it, but we feel the absence of it.'

We are also, I think it must be said, people who have known great sadness. Think of the desolation of the early settlers, their loneliness, their great ignorance of the land, their battles with it and, in most cases, their defeat and retreat into the cities.

Think, too, of the thousands of our young men slain in wars on the other side of the world, of the sorrows of the Great Depression of the 1930s and of the unemployed, the growing numbers of new poor, the middle class people sinking below the poverty line even today.

Is it any wonder, then, that we tend to suspect emotion and enthusiasm, that a wariness, an irony and often self-irony is one of our central characteristics? Like the hero of 'Waltzing Matilda', we have learned to travel light, emotionally at least.

So from the beginning we have felt ourselves called by the land. Joseph Furphy put it this way in *Such Is Life*: 'It is not in our cities or townships, it is not in our agricultural or mining areas that the Australian attains full consciousness of his (or her) nationality but here in the centre of the continent.'[1]

It is here, Furphy goes on, that we sense some 'unconfined, ungauged potentiality of resource', an 'ideographic prophecy which is inscribed in the land itself', a 'latent meaning' which it is our task to decipher. But this is also where problems arise, where the ambiguities in the definition of the word 'land' become important. Precisely because most of the people who have come to this country have been forced out from their own land, most of them, in the nineteenth century especially, had a great hunger for land, but land to be 'developed', to be farmed or grazed or mined for minerals to make us rich—not to live with, so much as to be made to work for us to fulfil the 'dream of great wealth got without exertion'[2] which drove the gold miners and prospectors.

In this sense Lawrence observed that Australia for us has not yet become a 'bride country', that we have rather raped it.[3] Certainly, the degradation of some of our most fertile farm and grazing land, the destruction of our forests, the salination of our creeks and rivers and the alarming decline of the water table, all suggest this.

But the wound is not just the land's. It is ours also. Many of us, it seems, have lost our sense of the sacred, the peace which for Australian Aboriginal people inheres in the land itself, and doing so, have fallen into the power of false gods: Mammon, the god of money; Moloch, the god of struggle, conflict and competition; and Marilyn Monroe, taken as the ikon of the destructiveness of the mindless pursuit of pleasure.

This became clear, for me at least, in 1979 at Noonkembah, Western Australia, when the mining company, Amax, wanted to drill for oil on an Australian Aboriginal sacred site. During the public debate those—and they were the majority—who supported the government, who insisted that Amax should go in and who conducted a paramilitary operation to see that they did so, argued either that the Australian Aboriginals had forfeited their right to the land since they had not 'developed' it—value being associated with economic profit—or that, following a neo-Darwinian line, the Australian Aboriginals were 'primitive' people, on the lowest rung of the evolutionary scale and doomed to die out and give way to 'civilization'—that is, to mining.

Apparently, they had no comprehension of the meaning of the word 'sacred'. The 'land' meant only an object to be exploited for economic purposes. At best we wanted, and perhaps still want, to turn this (for us) new land into a replica of the lands we had come from, planting European trees, forcing the land to bear European crops and building European-style cities and towns upon it. In this sense, as Laurie Duggan observes, pioneering represented a 'quest for normality'.[4]

This is understandable, of course. Most of the newcomers, in the nineteenth century especially, were in a state of culture-shock. The spiritual consequences, however, were destructive since this shrinking from the land entailed also a shrinking from difference, from the other. But the true God, as distinct from the gods we create according to our own image, is totally other, even though at the same time totally inner, the hitherto unknown truth of ourselves. As I see it, therefore, this shrinking from the otherness of the land is the other side of a shrinking from the otherness of God, from the call to go further, to realize as yet unknown possibilities within ourselves and our creation.

In this sense it is the equivalent of the Great Refusal for

which Dante castigated the Pope of his time, his indifference to the God of new possibility. Instead, we fear the land as he feared the claims of God, and subsequent mythology has given monumental status to this fear. Witness the fear of the land in much of our writing: in the 1880s Marcus Clarke, for example, argued that the 'dominant note' of the Australian landscape is a 'weird melancholy'[5] and to this day most Australians see the centre of Australia as a 'Dead Heart'. Others may see the Centre as an uncanny place, like a mother who will never give birth: the still-born. Refusing to commit ourselves to it, to the mystery of space, we cling to the fringe of ourselves as we cling to the fringes of the continent, or like Mr Bonner in Patrick White's *Voss*, we see Australia as the 'country of the future' in material terms, that is, of buildings, bridges and roads, expanding productivity, large bank balances and large needs.[6]

We find no place for our spirit in the land but rather desolation, like Sturt arriving at Lake Blanche in the Centre where he had hoped to find an inland sea. One of his party reported his reaction:

'The Captain feels most dreadfully chagrined. The scene is the climax of desolation; no trees, no shrubs, all bleak, barren, undulating sand. Miserable! Horrible!'[7] Sturt himself described it as a 'country not to be understood'. European eyes here saw only, in Marcus Clarke's words, 'the scribblings of nature learning to write'.

The book of nature, in which in Europe we read our own story and purposes, seemed closed to us here, a place without meaning or history. So the convict painter William Woolls complained in the 1820s that it was very difficult to paint here because there were no monuments, no stories of the past, no stories of heroic deeds. The truth is, as we are now coming to realize, that every inch of this land has a story and figures in the memory of a people who have lived here for 40,000 years or more!

In effect, then, by the large we non-Aboriginal Australians have refused or, better perhaps, have been unable to hear the call of the land to enter the land. We find it difficult, that is, to consider this second meaning of the word and to find *in* the land, not just a place, but a spiritual ocean. A place of the encounter with the living God who figures in the Exodus story as the desert God. In this story the desert becomes rather the place of the Covenant where the mutual bonding of God and his people is sealed. Nor is it accidental that this occurs in the desert, because the desert is the place above all others in which we come to the end of our human resources and are ready therefore to listen and to hear the call to go further, to move over the frontier of our limited reason, desires and purposes, into the vastness of God.

How, then, can we break out of the prison of our limitations, of our preoccupation with the false gods which is really a preoccupation with ourselves, living as we do 'distracted by distraction from distraction' in the consumer society which is perhaps one of the great confidence tricks of history, promising us happiness but actually bringing us death of the spirit as well as of the environment and thus of the land itself?

The answer, I believe, is both simple and difficult. Our failure is essentially imaginative on the one hand (we refuse to respond imaginatively to the land, interpreting it instead in a way which makes it the projection of our desires) and moral on the other (evil, as Matthew Fox has reminded us, is essentially the product of fear). For these reasons the remedy, too, lies in the imagination first of all and then in the will. For the reality is that since God exists, the call remains—God being in Eberhard Jüngel's fine phrase, 'the One Who Comes', whose being is his coming, his call, and remains in the land.[8]

The problem is one of interpretation; we are not able to read God there and interpret what seem to us merely the 'scribblings of nature learning to write'. We are unable to do so because our reading habits are limited. We are children of the Enlightenment, educated mainly in rationality, so we read for meaning rather than for presence. We 'read' the land in terms of our own projects for it, read it instrumentally, whereas the way we should read it is symbolically, for what it reveals, for how God speaks in and through it.

There is a power, as Ricoeur insists, in the symbol which calls to us, enlarges us. The symbol, he says, 'gives us to think'. It is, in a sense, therefore, a sacred place, because otherness, indeed the Other, speaks there, calls us out to reveal new possibilities to us, interrupting our complacencies. According to J. B. Metz, religion can best be described as interruption.[9] If we want therefore to read the depths of our experience of the land as place in its call to us to enter the land, the covenant with the living God, then the evidence of literature, the language of symbols, is very important, crucial even.

There are many texts we might use but let us choose one, set in the beginning time: Charles Harpur's *The Creek of the Four Graves*, written in the 1850s but written about the early days of the expansion into the interior, the 1820s and '30s. Its hero is the settler, Egremont, shown going into the wilderness to seek '. . . New streams and wider pastures for his fast increasing flocks . . .'[10], moving out in linear fashion into space seen as a kind of empty container through which he passes, but which it is also his task to fill and to possess for himself. Implicitly, he is an Abraham figure turned out from Eden into exile in this wilderness which is seen as somehow evil, the place of God's curse. The light on the leaves of the trees they pass, 'golden gleams', is compared to the glint of the sword of the Angel set to guard the gates of Paradise. The wilderness, therefore, is something apart from him, to be endured and if possible tamed on the way to the city God has promised. It is also felt as somehow evil: as the last light dies, they see a black cloud like a great black spider crawling across the sky. But it is the inhabitants of the wilderness, the Australian Aboriginals, who seem to be the embodiment of this evil. As the explorers sleep that night, a band of Aboriginals fall on them, killing them all except Egremont, who manages to escape. They are described thus:

'Hell's worst fiends burst howling up into the death-doomed world.'

They 'come in vengeance'[11] as, in the melodramatic imagination, evil comes to destroy the good.

This passage offers us a significant glimpse into the assumptions of the settlers: implicitly, they saw themselves as God's chosen people and the Australian Aboriginals as the people of the wilderness, people cursed by God who must be destroyed or at least conquered by and made to submit to the chosen people. But, unwittingly, at a deeper, more unconscious level, the imagery suggests that the settlers also recognized in the people of the land some creative force, some profound affinity with the living God, because they are shown leaping out of the fire, fire being crucially the symbol of the divine and of creativity.

Just as significantly, Egremont is terrified by the challenge they offer, the challenge the gospel as well as the mystical tradition insists on: that new life only comes out of death, the resurrection from the crucifixion. He flees from them, jumping first of all into a stream (in practical terms to prevent them tracking his foot prints) and then hiding in the earth in a cave on the creek bank — a cave, moreover, whose entrance is protected by roots which are compared with 'clammy snakes'.

To me at least, the symbolism is irresistible here: he has 'saved' himself by shrinking from the challenge, returning to the womb, 'homo incurvatus', turned in on himself and refusing the painful, dangerous but life-giving call to go into the land. As if to confirm this reading, the poem concludes on a cold, dead note, with the moon looking down on the faces of those who died, giving a sense not only of desolation but also of the emptiness of space and the human spirit's separation from it, set apart in our own world of frozen abstraction.

It might be an exaggeration to see in this a kind of foreshadowing of the alienation characteristic of our culture, the preoccupation with machines, objects and possessions and the profound indifferences, apathy and boredom of so many Australians living in a one-dimensional world, shut out from their own hearts. But there can be no doubt that there is in our culture a great reservoir of tears as yet untapped: the sorrows accumulated around the settlers who went out into the interior only to fail and to retreat into the cities and the thousands of dead slain in wars, the sufferings and humiliations of the Great

Depressions of the 1890s and 1930s and indeed, of those unemployed or otherwise victimized by the economic system today.

There is also a great loneliness, people shut inside themselves, unable to express their feelings or to communicate in depth with others, unable also to become part of the land — like the old man of Chaucer's *Pardoner's Tale* who is unable to die but wanders the earth, tapping the land with his staff, pleading, 'Love Moder, lette me inne' (Dear Mother, let me in).

That, then, is the negative aspect. But symbols also point us to a positive solution. As our unofficial national anthem, 'Waltzing Matilda' tells us, in our depths we are restless people, unable to settle down, 'wanderers on the way to the self'[12] longing to enter the land. Hence the spiritual fascination with the land, which is the paradoxical other side of our fear of it. Our deepest need, I suggest, is to enter the land to find the sacred place where we can enter into the mystery of God and thus of ourselves and of the land.

For this, however, we must go out once more into the wilderness and this time face the otherness, acknowledge the greatness it represents beyond ourselves, be prepared to undergo the ordeal at its hands, the initiation which we originally refused and continue to refuse. The churches in this country have perhaps forgotten or ignored the fact that, as Bonhoeffer puts it, there is no such thing as cheap grace, and that, to quote St John of the Cross this time, if you would go on the way to the All you must go by a way in which you have nothing.

It is for that reason that the physical fact of the desert as it appears to us may lead us to spiritual reality, to the recognition of the largeness and overpowering energy of the God who is, whose being for us is paradox, joy revealed in pain, life in death and presence in absence. A fine passage early in Finola Moorhead's wonderful novel, *Remember the Tarantella*, illustrates what I am trying to say here about the God of blessing who liberates us into his life by threatening to take it away. One of her characters, just escaped from prison, significantly finds herself in the desert:

> None walks here untouched... by the Never
> Never. Heat shimmers ahead taunting.
> The vast dome of the sky as solid as porcelain weighing, the
> perspective of distance is awry. Solid things like the
> pathetically thin rotors of a windmill near a bore appear like
> fantasies, a detail which is an omen, a cause.
> Few hold their own in such a landscape.[13]

The only people who hold their own are those prepared to acknowledge the limits of their own power, of their own reason, and to bow down in awe, drawn by the 'mysterium tremendum et fascinans', the sacred as that which is both terrifying and supremely fascinating. Here we understand the sheer audacity of existence, the wonder that life should exist at all where we in our arrogance find it so difficult to exist. To its Australian Aboriginal inhabitants, of course, the desert is fertile and life-giving because they can read its signs. We feel awe at its hidden abundance, at the low shrubs and wildflowers, the insects, the emus, the snakes and the lizards, all rejoicing in their own energies and possibilities. Its apparent emptiness gives the lie to all that we think we know and all the power we think we have.

It is this apparent emptiness which we must learn to lose, which draws us into itself or into the emptiness which is fed and then manifests itself as fullness. To enter it, however, we must learn to let go, to acknowledge our limits and our need, to pray as Moorhead's character does, seeing with the eyes of imagination and wonder, from the perspective which Creation Spirituality and contemporary science both offer.

> 'I am echo. I am emptiness. I observe.
> I am in the lonely bowl of the desert
> and eight feet from me is a bright
> Sturt desert pea. Here I can see to
> the end of the earth, for the big

world is a huge penny. The horizon
is a circle, not curve.'[14]

If mysticism is found in all cultures, it ought to belong very specially in Australia, for this is a land which compels silence, and the mystic (*mustes*) is one who is sworn to silence, drawn to a mystery which is essentially unspeakable, at least in words. To be silent, however, is not easy in a culture intent on achievement and full of idle chatter. Yet under the surface slickness of the consumer society we have become, of our absorption into the international media culture, there are signs of a longing for and an incipient awareness of the value of silence. The inarticulateness, the awkwardness of so many Australians, especially Australian men, may be the occasion of grace, the other side of a deep humility, of knowing one's place as someone finite and vulnerable, very small in contrast with the largeness of God, a largeness figured forth in the land itself.

True, this only half-conscious awareness is not often acknowledged—as Voss has it, we do tend to huddle on the fringes of ourselves as on the fringes of the continent. But where we do acknowledge the vulnerability, there is often a deep sense of compassion for ourselves as wounded people as well as for others. It may be then that we shall become truly ourselves when we learn to sorrow for our own woundedness, for our anxieties, hesitation and fears, our distrust of God and of this land, and thus also for all those whom these fears have led us to damage, especially our Australian Aboriginal brothers and sisters.

This will not be easy. But it is necessary, the hermeneutical principle for the proper interpretation of reality being, as Edward Schillebeecks says,[15] the scandal, the stumbling block, the painful rupture in the fabric of our lives which echoes the original explosion that gave creation life. In the first place, as we have said, this rupture, this scandal or stumbling block is the harshness of the land itself. But as we move into it, we will meet there the story of the first Australians, the Aboriginals, who lived so long and so worshipfully with, in, by and for the land. Meeting that, we will surely begin to realize the depth of our own woundedness, the fear, the clumsiness, the fumbling frivolity which governed our relations with them. For, like the land, they were different. They were 'others'. Unable to endure this otherness, we slew them, humiliated and dispossessed them because they would not become like us. In them, therefore, we meet the Suffering Servant who, precisely because he is 'wounded for our iniquities, bruised for our sins', is our liberator, pointing on the one hand to the results of our worship of false gods and on the other to the possibility of learning from the Australian Aboriginals to live differently, more in tune with the land and the rest of creation and, therefore, more prayerfully.

Essentially, then, the call by the land to enter the land is a call to conversion, to a change in our way of living, a call to become friends of the earth, of its creatures and of all peoples who share this one life with us on this small and very vulnerable planet suspended against the backdrop of infinite space. It is significant, I think, that our great writer and prophet, Patrick White, in the two novels which deal most directly with this call from the land to enter the land, *Voss* and *A Fringe of Leaves*, sees the Australian Aboriginals as the instruments of this conversion.

This is not the place, however, to rehearse his argument, only to conclude with his words when he returned to Australia. He returned, he said, because he saw in the land itself a call to the 'state of silence, simplicity and humility which is the only proper state for the artist as for the human being'.[16]

We are not Aboriginals but newcomers, migrant people who must learn the secret of this state—learning it, however, not just from Australian Aboriginals but by coming to accept and love and forgive ourselves even in our woundedness. For Christians the only way to gain new life, to enter into the fullness of creation, remains the Way of the Cross.

NOTES

1. Furphy, J., *Such is Life*, Lloyd O'Neil, Melbourne, 1971, pp 80–1.

2. Richardson, H. H., *Australian Felix*, Penguin, Melbourne, p 8.
3. Lawrence, D. H., *Kangaroo*, Penguin, Melbourne, p 9.
4. Duggan, L., *The Ash Range*, Picador, Sydney, 1987, p 9.
5. Clarke, M., *Poems of Adam Lindsay Gordon*: quoted in Turner, I. (ed), *The Australian Dreaming*, Sun Books, Melbourne, 1968, p 102.
6. White, P., *Voss*, Penguin, Melbourne, 1971, p 349.
7. Smith, D., 'Dick Smith's Journey of Discovery and Adventure', *Australian Geographic*, Vol 1, January/March, 1986, p 36.
8. Jungel, E., *God As the Mystery of the World*, Grand Rapids, Michigan
9. Metz, J. B., *Faith In History and Society*, Crossroads/Seabury, New York, 1980, p 171.
10. Ackland, M. (ed), *Charles Harpur Selected Poetry and Prose*, Penguin, Melbourne, 1986, p 140.
11. Ibid., p 145.
12. Chisholm, A. R. & Quinn, J. J. (eds), *The Prose of Christopher Brennan*, Angus & Robertson, Sydney, 1965, p 45.
13. Moorhead, F., *Remember the Tarantella*, Primavera Press, Sydney, 1987, p 5.
14. Ibid.
15. Schillebeecks, E., *Christ: The Christian Experience in the Modern World*, SCM Press, London, 1982, p 35.
16. White, P., *The Prodigal Son* and *Australian Letters*, 1, 3, April 1958, p 39.

Living In a Unitary Age

KEVIN TRESTON

As I write this reflection about a new age of consciousness, I am reminded of a recent phone call in which the concerned Christian spoke of his anxiety about the consequences of 'New Age' thinking on the Christian churches. The term 'New Age' is a distracting one for the emerging era of consciousness. For many people, 'New Age' evokes images of crystals, tarots, channeling, planetary processions, chakras and drugs. Many of these New Age expressions are actually a rediscovery of ancient wisdoms about human existence. However, a general perception of New Age is one of the esoteric or even the bizarre.

What is happening is too serious to be dismissed as belonging to the lunatic fringe. Unitary age consciousness has exciting possibilities for the future of humankind and we should seize the opportunity to creatively respond to the challenges posed by the onset of the Unitary Age. We are living in an intermediary period and are entering an unknown forest with untold invitations to create a new world.

Unitary Age
I have chosen the term 'Unitary Age' to describe this phase in the evolution of consciousness because the word 'unitary' best expresses the core of the meaning of this era. 'Unitary' indicates the acknowledgment of the interconnections and integration

of all things within a pluriformity of life. The problem with the more popular term of 'New Age' is that many of its manifestations are not new at all but a return to recover past traditions. The name 'unitary' captures the essence of this new age by denoting the convergence of many elements of our living into a new unity of wholeness.

By 'Unitary Age' consciousness, I mean a growing awareness of all things in our universe and a quest for interiority which is a simplication of a search for holistic spirituality. The movement towards spirituality is integral to the awakening of a global vision towards our world. In the Unitary Age, humankind is poised for a great leap in the psyche and spirit. Teilhard de Chardin wrote: 'We are inevitably approaching a new age in which the world will throw off its chains and at last give itself up to the power of its inner affinities.' Peter Russell rather dramatically states: 'Humanity could be on the threshold of an evolutionary leap, a leap which could occur in a flash of evolutionary time, a leap such as occurs only once in a billion years. And the changes leading to this leap are taking place right before our eyes, or rather behind them within our minds.'[1]

Four Eras
If one tries to view the gradual unfolding of human consciousness over the millions of years, the 'Unitary Age' might be regarded as the fourth stage in its evolution. The four major movements in the historical development of consciousness are:

(1) Tribal Age
   From the beginning of human life to about 5000 BCE

(2) Agricultural Age
   From about 5000 BCE until 1600 CE

(3) Scientific Age or Industrial Age
   From 1600 CE to 1960 CE

(4) Unitary Age
   From 1960 CE

Tribal Age

During the tribal era, men and women lived in a world suffused with meaning. Each aspect of the living world was woven into meaning by myths and rituals. The mystery of the world was explained in sacred stories. Divine spirits, some friendly, others hostile, were present in every phase of life. Shamanistic leaders articulated the meaning systems and were mediators between the spirits and the community.

Agricultural Age

In the agricultural era, society became more differentiated according to social class and status. At least four social groups emerged: royalty, military, religious-cultic groups or elders and the farmers. In the latter stages of this era, a merchant class appeared. One of the features of the agricultural epoch was a strictly ordered hierarchy of authority patterns based on a patriarchical model. During this time, religious systems began to appear where the gods were controlled by scriptures, cults, rituals and tradition.

Scientific Age

The scientific age was characterized by an explosion of information about the world. During the latter part of this era, change happened at such speed that writers spoke of 'future shock'. An example of the speed of change is illustrated by the rapid development in flying. Within sixty years of learning to fly, astronauts had landed on the moon. The shadow side of the scientific phase was the disintegration of a coherent cosmology and the emergence of a mechanistic view of the world. Humankind became divorced from the earth and became dominators and exploiters, rather than partners and responsible stewards.

The specialization of knowledge, which was a necessary feature of scientific development, resulted in an erosion of a unified vision of the universe. Nature was like a big clock with myriads of minute parts all following Newtonian laws of physics. The earth was considered as a deposit of natural resources readily available for human exploitation. However, the insatiable appetites of technology and industry so rapidly consumed the earth's resources that within two hundred years of the beginning of the industrial revolution, there are warning signs that our earth is becoming tired and exhausted.

During the latter part of the twentieth century, it was increasingly obvious that humankind was rushing towards an ecological disaster unless it reversed its attitudes towards the earth. The myth of unlimited progress has been exposed as a sham. Events such as the Holocaust, the Depression, the World Wars, and the arsenal of nuclear weaponry have jolted the world into a realization that the demonic face of technology threatens the very existence of life on earth. The quest for a new story to live more harmoniously with our earth has become a greater imperative, especially with the partial collapse of traditional symbols associated with a coherent meaning system.

Why did the Unitary Age occur now?

A number of social, religious and economic influences converged into a powerful stream of consciousness which provoked new thinking about the future of humankind in its relationship to the earth and cosmos.

Gap between rich and poor

The growing gulf between rich and poor countries is stark evidence of the farce of international accountability in the utilization of resources. Today one quarter of the world's five billion people live below the poverty line and the world's population is expected to exceed eight billion within the next forty years. The prospect of massive poverty and seething social resentment on a world scale is a social and economic reality to be addressed by the world community. The report of the World Commission on Environment and Development — Our Common Future described many of the urgent changes needed to counter the downward spiral in the quality of life for many people. The report warned that the rate of change is outstripping the ability of scientific disciplines and our current capabilities to assess and advise. The nations of the world have no option but to devise alternative ways of distributing the resources of the earth if they wish to arrest the dichotomy between rich and poor. The well documented evidence of widespread pollution, acid rain, erosion, toxic wastes and deforestation focused attention on our earth, which is being brought to its knees by abuse and pillage. Humankind has to discover a new story for the earth before it is too late. The industrial story must be discarded or at least be transformed as a symbol to convey meaning about our existence.

A growing feminine consciousness is restoring the imbalance in sexual complementarity. It is no coincidence that rape of the earth occurs with oppression of women. Patriarchy needs to be rejected as an affront to harmonious relationships with our world. The feminine movement has proposed alternative ways of participating in our social system without a superior/inferior dualism as the norm for our perceptions about social reality.

Christians are slowly awaking from a long winter of hibernation about care for the earth. No longer locked into an afterlife focus and dualistic view of body/soul dichotomy, many Christians are beginning to see stewardship of the earth as integral to their fidelity to God's covenant. During the 1980s the mainline Christian churches became actively allied with the ecological movement. The Assembly theme of the World Council of Churches Assembly in 1991 in Canberra was: 'Come Holy Spirit—Renew the Whole Creation'. The conference seeks to explore the coming of the new creation for the world through the Spirit and our cooperative endeavors.

Modern scientific theorists, such as Lovelock, Sheldrake, Kuhn, Jantsch and Capra, propose paradigms of the universe which emphasize interdependence and mutual dependence on all other life forms. Science supports the holistic care movement. There are many signs in our contemporary world that we are discarding theories about the world which were mechanistic and more appropriate to an industrial consciousness. During the latter part of the twentieth century, interest in the Western world began to move from control of the material world to the uncharted field of the human psyche.

What are features of a Unitary Age?
I suggest a number of characteristics of the Unitary Age.

1. Partnership with the Earth

The most obvious aspect of the Unitary Age is an attitude of partnership with the earth. The wanton use of earth's resources has raised many questions about our lifestyles and about how long humankind expects to continue its current rate of using resources before the earth is exhausted. The Amazon forest, the largest rainforest area in the world, will become extinct as a rainforest by 2020 unless the process of deforestation is stopped. Some of the trends in ecological destruction are almost irreversible. It is estimated that at the present rate of the death of species, twenty-five per cent of all the earth's species will become extinct by 2010.

The Unitary Age recalls us to a faithfulness to the first covenant (Genesis, Chapter 9). In the covenant formula, God specifies the covenant is one between God, us and the earth. God invites us to the restoration of harmonious relationships.

The implications of the first covenant are far reaching. Humankind now possesses the capacity to modify the life-sustaining processes of the earth. In Unitary Age consciousness, we are becoming more aware of the interactive nature of all life, not just human life. To be pro-life is to be concerned about the affirmation of all life on the universe, not just the life of 'homo sapiens'.

The Bible is ambivalent about our relationship with the earth. One Jewish tradition was tentative about the kind of relationships we should have with nature because nature could be a source of sin through participation in the fertility rites of neighboring cultures. Christians inherited a Jewish concern about limiting the transcendence of God through fertility rituals which were conducted in sacred forests and mountain sites. The elimination of all fertility rites from the Jewish–Christian tradition tended to banish the integral nature of sexuality and procreation from a holistic view of creation.

An alternative Jewish tradition celebrated God's revelation

in creation. The Hebrew people believed that God's revelation was to be discovered in the book of the scriptures and the book of nature. The seas, mountains, and all life forms around us can provoke us to wonder and awe. The sacrament of the cosmos is an invitation to enter mystery. Tragically the injunction to humankind to have dominion over the earth (Genesis 1: 28) has been perverted in its meaning by a fundamentalist interpretation to rationalize the rape of the earth. The command of Yahweh is to be responsible stewards.

Through the two thousand years of the Christian story, the followers of Jesus have never easily resolved this inheritance of ambivalence towards the earth. The most persistent heresies in church history have been dualistic ones which exalted the superiority of the soul over the body. The eschatological orientation towards heaven influenced many Christians to form a detached or even indifferent attitude towards the fate of the world.

'Saving one's soul' was considered the prime objective of the Christian life. Christian thinking was deeply affected by Platonic philosophy which regarded the spirit as the essence of our being. Thomas Berry commented on this approach to the world: 'Human perfection was thought of as detachment from the phenomenal world in favor of the divine eternal world, which was presented as our true destiny.'[2]

In fairness to Christianity, it should be noted that there was always an assumption in Christian doctrine that creation was a foundational tenet of faith. The sacramentality of the world as revealing God's presence is celebrated in liturgy, song and worship. The pages of the Christian story tell of many 'creation people' such as Francis of Assisi, Julian of Norwich, Hildegard of Bingen, the Rhineland mystics, Thomas Berry, Teilhard de Chardin, Matthew Fox, and the monks who cared for God's creation through their farming and husbandry.

The Black Death (1349 CE) left a deep mark on the Christian consciousness about the earth. Death seemed to strike at random and with savage power. Christians were further weakened in responding to the world by the bitter religious divisions of the sixteenth and seventeenth centuries. Religious wars absorbed the energies of the churches and left them ill prepared to dialog with the burgeoning scientific revolution and its new understanding of the world. Christian theology emphasized redemption, rather than creation. The formulation of the doctrine of original sin in the fifth century reinforced a negative perspective on humankind and creation.

In his famous seminal essay, 'The Historical Roots of our Ecological Crises', Lynn White[3] blamed Christianity for the ecological crises. His thesis proposed that Western culture has been shaped by the Christian ethic and this ethic towards the earth is one of exploitation and domination. White claimed that Christianity teaches a path to salvation which is external to nature.

White's thesis is worthy of careful study. However I believe his view is too simplistic in its conclusions. Our world offers tragic evidence of the plunder of the earth in many countries whose cultures are not formed by a Christian ethic.

The earth is an interconnected ecosystem. Each part, however small, touches our lives in some way, however indirect. Modern scientific theories such as the 'Gaia' hypothesis of Lovelock, describe the intricate pattern of relationships between every feature of the earth. After four hundred years of learning about the parts of our universe, we are beginning to appreciate the whole.

The first European settlers to Australia were products of the philosophy and ethics of the industrial era. They were bewildered by the seasons and the land. In contrast, the first Australian people constructed their symbolic meaning system from their relationships with the earth. European settlements tended to cling precariously to the edge of the vast strange continent. The bush was to be penetrated and conquered. As wealth began to flow back to Europe, the myth of the bush was born where true mateship was forged when people stuck together to beat the loneliness and hardship of the outback. The earth was to be subdued if Australia was to become rich.

Today over eighty per cent of Australians live in six urban

areas, making Australia one of the most urbanized countries in the world. However, the popularity of swimming, camping, outdoor holidays, beaches, gardening and bush safaris attest to the yearnings of many Australians to be reconnected to the earth. Environmental issues win or lose elections. No politician can afford to ignore the 'green' vote. Australians, like so many in the world, are searching for meaning, for a symbolic system which connects us to our earth. How this symbolic system can be reconciled with the values and symbols of a technological society is a complex question. Perhaps this quest of recon-ciliation can be assisted by coming to our first people as humble learners and listeners to the lessons of the Dreamtime.

A basic theme in Unitary Age consciousness is a holistic approach to the world where we live creatively with the earth as partner. Humankind cannot deny its gifted place in the universe but its identity is in giving as well as receiving, in living as stewards who recognize the earth as having rights to life. Human life is not at the expense of other living organisms.

2. Contemplation and Sabbath

One of my favourite Zen stories is about a monk who was galloping down the road with his robes flapping in the wind. An old farmer, sitting on the gate, yelled out as the monk clattered by: 'Sir, where are you going?' The monk shouted back: 'Don't ask me, ask the horse!' Our culture is one of a high incidence of noise. Car radios, television, jackhammers, car traffic and blaring transistors fill our airwaves, clamoring for our attention. The ceaseless chatter of our culture seems to hide a deep inner terror of silence.

In the biblical story, the sabbath or seventh day is the day on which the various strands of creation are woven together through contemplation. On the seventh day, God rested and saw that what God had made was good, very good. Our work-orientated Western world has identified with the six–day work-ing God and conveniently relegated the seventh day as a kind of after-thought of God's creative activity. However, work without insight is a sentence to a treadmill of labor. This kind of compulsive work is bondage. The biblical sabbath is the day of a new exodus in which we are invited to move from slavery to freedom. In the gospel of Luke, Jesus commences his ministry on the sabbath by announcing a new time of freedom (Luke 4:16ff).

Unless we discover quiet spaces, we cannot descend to the refreshing wells of the Spirit. Contemplation opens doors to the Source of all creation. Through the sabbath, we become listeners to the breathing of the universe. The search for unity within our being is linked with the experience of harmonious relationships with all creation. Living in a constant throb of noise dulls us to the prospect of being surprised by the genius of the artist Creator. In the words of Walter Burghardt, contemplation is 'taking a long, loving look at what is real'.[4]

Meister Echkhart writes: 'Nothing in all creation is so like God as stillness.'[5] When we are locked into a circuit of activity, we become less vulnerable to the beauty and trauma of creation.

The wilderness is a powerful symbol of contemplative creation. Joseph Meeker describes this symbol: 'Wilderness is a complex of natural relationships where plants, animals and land collaborate to fulfill their environments without technological human interference.'[6] As wilderness is essential for planetary functioning, so is a retreat into wilderness an imperative journey for humankind. Sometimes we need to be dispossessed of our securities and be challenged to resituate our egos within a proper context of world. In the wilderness, the Jewish people were bonded into a community. Jesus entered the wilderness to discern the style of his ministry. During his sojourn in the wilderness, he was confronted by three temptations to misuse power (Matthew 4:1–11). Through discernment, Jesus chose the way of humble service.

One of the features of Unitary Age consciousness is an expanding awareness of our psyche and spirituality. Sabbath and contemplation enable us to go beyond induced consumer needs to explore the paths of the Gospel child (Matthew 18:2). The pursuit of the simple life within the complexities of a technological society sets us free from the tyranny of social compulsions and expectations.

3. Global Vision

After the sixteenth century, humankind lost its ongoing vision of the universe. The industrial revolution and enlightenment movements separated mind from matter. Newtonian laws of physics suggested a mechanistic view of the universe. Francis Bacon, regarded as the father of modern science, stated that the earth is tortured until it yields up its secrets. We owe so much to Bacon and the scientists for unlocking so many of the earth's secrets. However the process of reductionism, by which everything is reduced to its smallest parts in order that the part might be properly studied, limited our grasp of the holistic nature of the world. Through reductionism, the planet is perceived as a series of small isolated laboratories in which scientists conduct experiments. Excessive specialization in science eroded a unified vision of the world and paid little attention to the ethical implications of research.

Positivism was another element in the scientific era. Positivism emphasized the reality of what can be observed and measured. It ignored a mystical and numinous appreciation of the universe. God was banished to the realm of superstition because God could not fit under a microscope. The belief in the earth as an expression of God's revelation vaporized in the test tubes of scientific analysis.

However the scientific revolution also generated an intense interest in a global perspective. Technological advances in communications and transport provided the means to create global awareness. The horrors of the World Wars, the Depression and nuclear weapons brought home the realization of how fragile are relationships in our world. Territoriality and separateness are luxuries which are detrimental to the welfare of our ecological health. The recent scientific theories have described the earth as a living organism in a constant process of self renewal. The General Systems of Miller (1978) argued that everything in the universe belongs to a system and each sub-system works towards harmony.

Unfortunately the Western world has become so conditioned to specialization that our society has become dysfunctional.[7] We laugh (or cry) at the absurdity of a newspaper report that seven people are involved in the changing of a light bulb in Parliament House, Canberra. Demarcation disputes among unions would be comical if they were not so destructive to the flagging economy.

Current scientific theories about the vital significance of chaos in creation remind us that our global vision needs to integrate the cycle of life and death within our understanding of a dynamic universe. The universe is not obedient. Our world is not a meek follower of human specified laws. Brian Swinne writes: 'Scientists have discovered that an unbridgeable surprise is at the centre of things... almost nothing would be more surprising than modern scientists discovering surprise.'[8]

A holistic vision of the universe is not one of a pseudo-harmonious world in which all is lovely in the rose garden. Our global perspective is one where opposites are reconciled. St Paul acknowledged the integral place of suffering in creation: 'We are well aware that the whole of creation, until this time, has been groaning in labor pains (Romans 8:22).' The 'via negativa' is essential to the journey of the heart. Cross and resurrection are two faces of the one cosmic Christ.

The Taoist teachings about 'yin' and 'yang' offer a way of incorporating suffering within our life story. The polar opposites of 'yin' and 'yang' become absorbed into a unity through the transformation of each other. The dualism of energies must be brought into a unity and not differentiated into competing and alienating parts.[9] Jung's idea of befriending the 'shadow' on the journey of individuation is another way of describing this incorporation.

The 'angst' of our contemporary society, with its attendant feeling of alienation, is generated by a lack of a unifying focus for its 'yin' and 'yang' creative energies. Instead of a movement towards the source of unity in the Divine Spirit, the opposites are projected into a frenetic quest for material goods, status or violence. The paradise garden as the archetypal symbol of unity through harmony is dissipated when de-creation is not intentionally integrated into our creation story.

The Western world's obsession with certainty and objectivity has made a significant contribution to the explosion of knowledge and technology, but it has failed to grasp that an authentic understanding of the world necessarily includes the dimensions of chaos and uncertainty. A global vision will resituate humankind within nature, not outside it. Such a vision will bring some coherence to the divergent and competing movements in technology. Ultimately we will realize we have one earth, one home.

4. Just Society

We live in an interconnected universe. Any particular life system is in some way dependent on cooperative interactions with other species. Human beings have been commissioned as stewards of nature who have the social responsibility to gather and share in justice the resources of the earth for the nurturing of the whole ecosystem. The first covenant was an affirmation of this ideal. The sad reality is society is being divided between a wealthy technocratic class and non-skilled workers who are being displaced by rapid advances in technology. The two dominant economic systems, capitalism and Marxism, both reduce people to the status of disposable economic units.

One could cite many examples of resources being squandered. One instance is that half of the world's scientists are presently engaged in war-related industries. Every minute, two million dollars are spent on the production and use of armaments. At the risk of arousing the ire of the conservationists, one might also wonder about the rescue of two whales trapped in the ice at the cost of millions of dollars while so many children die of malnutrition.

A characteristic of the Unitary Age is an urgent quest for an alternative economic system which is sustainable. By a sustainable economy, I mean one in which all life forms are reverenced and enhanced. The concept of sustainable economy implies that resources are utilized prudently to safeguard future generations. The earth is a faithful bookkeeper who will call us to account. Our own sense of accountability to the world community will insist that we go beyond individualism to respect the sanctity of all life.

No one individual or nation has the right to experience a lifestyle which ignores the rights of others or deprives people of the right to food, shelter, education and basic justice. The earth is not a bottomless pit of resources but rather a delicate ecosystem which is struggling to service the incessant demands on its strained resources.

In Unitary Age consciousness, there is a growing resolve to anchor technology within the context of how we relate to our world. We now assert that technology is an instrument for humankind's benefit. It cannot be a tyrannical master.

Justice is concerned with the restoration of right relationships with each other and the earth. The movement towards a just society necessarily involves a process of collaboration among people, communities and nations. No one group, such as scientists or business leaders, should be able to dictate the priorities of an economic system. Our leaders need to exercise power for justice so that the quality of life for everyone will be enhanced.

The psychologist, Rollo May, has named five kinds of power: exploitative, competitive, manipulative, integrative and nurturing. When we exercise power which is exploitative, competitive or manipulative, we are using power to defeat others and control them. In Unitary Age consciousness, we are committed to expressions of power which empower others to realize their gifts and to be challenged to imagine that our world could be a different place for justice.

A particular form of perverted power is patriarchy. A patriarchal society is inherently unjust because it assumes that male norms are the criteria for setting values in society. Patriarchy assumes that male leadership is a divinely ordained precept. Such a view still blights the Christian story with its scandalous shadow and betrays the radical stance of Jesus towards women.

The subjugation of the female by the male epitomizes the

racial, social and religious oppressions in every culture. Feminist writers propose that patriarchy underpins all forms of domination. The marriage of patriarchy with industrialization further marginalized women in the industrial era, because the feminine role was relegated to the non-monetary role in the domestic household.

The new consciousness of the Unitary Age insists that the voices of women be attended to in the halls of power where societal decisions are taken.

5. Spirituality

Religious historians tell us that religion as an organized social system is a relatively recent phenomena in the long history of human development. Religious rituals were being celebrated by 50,000 BCE but it was not until about 2,500 BCE that major religions began to appear in a recognized structure. The formalization of religion allowed humans to confine the divine to institutional structures.[10] The divisive religious struggles after the sixteenth century weakened the influence of Christianity to affect the direction of the emerging industrial society. Spirituality retreated to the private domain of each individual Christian. Commitment to social justice was minimal except as charity to the oppressed through such groups and people as John Wesley, Colonel Booth and the religious congregations.

As the institutionalized churches became less relevant to the aspirations of Western society so did the masses react against formalized religion. The religious vacuum was quickly filled by such ideologies as capitalism, socialism, communism, fascism, nationalism and consumerism. To a great extent, the religious scene in the Western world was indeed a land of broken symbols.

The 1960s witnessed a new quest for spirituality. Radical and alternative expressions of new age spiritualities thrust into prominence a bewildering series of gurus and practices, such as channeling, palmistry, crystals and chakra healing. Keen devotees rushed from one seminar to another in search of the latest spiritual elixir. Within the Catholic Church, the leaders assembled at the Second Vatican Council (1962–1965) to face urgent renewal issues.

A casual observer of new age spirituality may too easily dismiss its manifestations as aberrations of an authentic search for ultimate meaning. However a more careful look at these movements will discern a profound wisdom in new age religions; they emphasize the interrelatedness of all things in the cosmos and the unity of body and Spirit. Ellwood states: 'Fundamental to this world view . . . is the realization that physical and spiritual power and meaning coexist everywhere and can be tapped, not just by faith and prayer but also by gnosis or wisdom and by informed psycho-spiritual technique.'[11]

I would now like to identify some key features of Unitary Age spirituality and suggest the challenges which these features pose for Christian churches.

(i) Contemporary spirituality must take the world seriously and become more actively involved in a quest for justice. Unitary Age spirituality involves a conversion to the consequences of the first covenant between God, us and the earth.

(ii) The search of scholars for the historical Jesus has distracted us from an exploration of what the cosmic Christ means to Christian faith and to creative dialog with those who ask religious questions. The primal myth is Jesus and new creation through the inauguration of the Kingdom of God needs to be restored as a reference point for renewal of church life and its pastoral mission. The Kingdom symbol should be a unifying symbol. It should not be one which is used to rationalize sectarianism or religious imperialism.

The movement from the dogmatic Christ to the Cosmic Christ will empower Christian communities to live in reverence with other groups who drink from other wells of God's revelation. In particular, the journey for the 'Atman,' the God beyond all divine images, will invite us to be attentive companions to the first people of our various countries, such as Australian Aboriginals, Maoris, native Indians.

Christ is both Redeemer and Reminder. Christ the Reminder recalls the face of a God who is compassionate. As Reminder, Christ affirms our humanity as daughters and sons of God.

(iii) The honoring of our world will lead Christian people to work in collaboration with other agencies of the community to care for all life forms on the planet.

(iv) The journey towards spiritual wholeness in the Unitary Age will encourage people to celebrate the fullness of life (John 10:10). Addictions such as drugs, excessive alcohol, materialism and individualism, have to be resisted. Holistic spirituality integrates the ancient wisdoms of such movements as Tai-Chi, yoga, pranic healing and aromatherapy.

(v) Unitary Age spirituality is mystical because it seeks to bring oneness to the core of our being with God. Love is the energizing force to generate life. Mysticism draws together the strands of love into a unity with the Source of Love. The Trinity as the oneness of God in a relationship of love is the primal paradigm of Unitary Age spirituality.

(vi) A Unitary Age consciousness will critique the power structures of society and church to ensure that the expressions of power are conducive to setting people free. If the exodus is the foundational Jewish-Christian myth, then any dominant/subordinate model of relationships is to be resisted. A new creation will not occur by decrees and commands but by a conversion of hearts to a unitary vision of the world where compassion, vulnerability and empowerment are features of leadership.

(vii) Unitary Age spirituality draws from the heritage of thousands of years of responses to the great religious question about ultimate meaning. We are being led into a spirituality which affirms that the earth and human beings are to form a single living community. Our knowledge and reverence of the past story will shape our paths of future discoveries. Like the scribe in Matthew's gospel we will be house-holders who bring out from storerooms of spirituality 'things both old and new' (Matthew 13:52).

The seven elements of Unitary Age spirituality offer significant themes for its direction.

CONCLUSION

The enormous advances in our knowledge and information have transformed the way we perceive our place in the world and construct images to reflect our reality. In this emerging era of consciousness, the Unitary Age, humankind is being impelled towards a holistic and global vision of the world. Such a vision will invite us into collaboration with others to preserve our planetary system, to combat divisive economic and social systems which are debilitating the quality of all life forms in the universe. We can resist the onset of this new age by ignoring its clear signs or we can respond creatively to its challenges.

For religious people, a faith position postulates that God is moving through this giant leap in consciousness. God is inviting us to become partners and co-creators to celebrate the pluriformity of life in all its diversity.

NOTES
1. Russell, P., *The Awakening Earth: Our Next Evolutionary Leap*, Rutledge & Kegan Paul, London, 1982, p vii. Quoted from: O'Murchu, D. (1987), *Coping with Change in the Modern World*, The Mercier Press, Dublin, p 16.
2. Berry, T., 'Economics: Its Effect on the Life Systems of the World' in Lonergan, A. & Richards, E. E. (eds), *Thomas Berry and the New Cosmology*, Twenty Third Publications, Mystic CT, 1988, p 16.
3. White, L., 'The Historical Roots of our Ecological Crises', *Science*, March 10, 1967, pp 1203–1207.
4. Burghardt, W. J. 'Contemplation: A Long Loving Look at What is Real', *Praying*, March-April, 1990.
5. Fox, M., *Original Blessings*, Bear & Co., Santa Fe, 1984, p 133.
6. Meeker, J. W., 'Wisdom and Wilderness', *Creation*, May/June 1989, p 22.
7. O'Murchu, D., *Coping with Change in the Modern World*, The

Mercier Press, Dublin, 1987, p 58.
8. Swinne, B., 'Is the Universe Obedient?', *Creation*, Nov/Dec 1988, p 22.
9. Cooper, J. C., *Yin and Yang, The Taoist Harmony of Opposites*, The Aquarian Press, 1981, p 15.
10. Bellah, R., *Beyond Belief*, Harper & Row, New York, 1970.
11. Ellwood, R. S., 'The New Age and a New World: A Social Perspective,' *The Catholic World*, May/June 1989, p 113.

To Sacred Origins —
Through Symbol
and Story

ELIZABETH CAIN

Acknowledging ourselves as 'friends of creation', we may be aware, and with some hope, that the global village built by humanity is undergoing some radical change. We have witnessed the great movements of the human spirit in Eastern Europe, the toppling of despots, and the capitulation of governments to the power of those who work to preserve and restore the earth rather than exploit it. These are small beginnings, but it seems that almost suddenly there is a breaking through of a global awareness that it is time, and high time, to begin to build a new world. Could the 1990s become a decade of hope and peace?

And the gathering of people who call themselves 'friends of creation' is also a sign of hope for our universe. We are honored that Matthew Fox and Joanna Macy should come to Australia to lead us further into living a spirituality of passion and compassion that is creation-centered. Another incredibly rich resource that we have is ourselves, Australian people who belong in this ancient land and share in its story. For, among other things, this is a time of exploration and a revelation of those great patterns or motifs that have come together to form the uniqueness of who we are as a people and as individuals.

Such an exploration can only begin and be centered in the land, in creation, and always the quality of relationship between people and land is an accurate gauge of that people's capacity for a true spiritual awareness. Those who love and reverence the earth have, as it were, an 'instinct for mystery' or an instinct for the sacred, the lived knowledge that the divine is the inscape of all that is.

There is at present a fast-growing awareness and an increasing articulation of the myriad expressions of the Australian experience. There is a flourishing market for Australian writing, film and art forms, whether they celebrate the natural untamed beauty of the landscape, or with outrage mourn the destruction of the wilderness. There is a growing awareness of the sheer horror of the pain in the history of the Australian Aboriginal people at the hands of the white European. Australian Aboriginal paintings are becoming known, and there is a sense of wonder as some Australians are beginning to glimpse what our European forebears had no eyes to see.

There is an opening out of awareness to the experience of women in the Australian story, celebrated and commiserated in books like Eve Pownall's *Australian Pioneer Women*,[1] or Drusilla Modjeska's *Inner Cities*[2] — Australian women's memory of place.

For Geoffrey Blainey, Australia is 'a land half-won'[3] still carrying much extraneous cultural baggage, and Robert Hughes explores the arrival of convicts in Australia, from their perspective, as the coming to A *Fatal Shore*.[4]

Autobiographies have increased, and people like John Colmer are concerned with 'autobiography as an art'. One such is Sally Morgan's My *Place*,[5] another *The Puzzles of Childhood*, in which Manning Clark writes of memory as his way of moving out of darkness into light.[6]

One of the most expressive of the images which attempts to capture something of the spirituality of a people who were, and in some cases still are the living embodiment of a creation-centered spirituality, is Bruce Chatwin's *Songlines* —'the song-lines stretching across the continents and ages; there wherever people have trodden they have left a trail of song... The songlines emerge as invisible pathways connecting up all over Australia; ancient tracks made of songs which tell of the creation of the land.'[7]

Many of the songlines of the more immediate rootedness of the European Australian were sung in the Celtic tradition, a tradition of extraordinary richness which has an undeniable affinity with the Dreaming of the Australian Aboriginal. The Celts lived 'between worlds', having the capacity to see with the inner eye as well as the outer. Their sacred stories were woven and sung by the bard, and they lived in union with the spirits of trees, rocks and animals. Life together was family-based, tribal, and non-hierarchical, and in the Celt was the 'peregrinatione', the wanderer, the one who went off into the desert or the wilderness. And there was Brigid, the virgin earth mother, the fruitful one, the one who kept fire of hearth and fire of heart burning.

It has seemed to me that the claiming of my Celtic heritage may be a stepping stone taking me into the Australian Aboriginal Dreaming with an immediacy I could not otherwise know.

Although individuals among the early white settlers and their descendants have in some way found and sung their songlines, and have made their dream journeys, a society which is motivated by fear and greed is like an environment which stifles and kills the free flow of spirit in the universe. In such an environment the finding of the songlines cannot happen easily. But, as Australians we have been given something precious, a people who know and have sung their songlines, and in whom something of those songlines still exists. I believe that if we are to learn and live a creation-centered spirituality in Australia, a primary source of the wisdom we need must be the wisdom of the Dreaming, the claiming and celebration of our own aboriginality.

There is a memory that still brings tears to my eyes, a day of rebirth in January, 1988, when a decimated people gathered together from all over Australia and marched as Australians. They said to us all, 'We have survived'. May we learn to treasure these gentle people, and come to know with T. S. Eliot that humility is the only wisdom we can hope to gain.[8]

In exploring a creation-centered spirituality as it might be lived in the Australian context, the Aboriginal 'Dreaming' in its mythology and the energies in the sacred sites wait to be reclaimed as a deep imprint in the very structure of our hearts and minds. We must learn to touch into our latent capacities to move into the dreaming parts of ourselves and our land, in order that the myth or sacred story of our being may break into lived awareness.

We may think of the Aboriginal Dreaming as our root and foundation as Australians, for that is what it is. While the origins of land and people are largely hidden from our awareness, the language of the Dreaming in myth, art, song and dance, can give glimpses not only of an ancient land, but of the beliefs of a people whose very understanding of existence was forged in that most fundamental of all relationships, that between person or people, and land.

As we continue to wound a land already in agony, we may hear Arkady in *Songlines* say that for the Aboriginal, 'To wound the earth is to wound yourself, and if others wound the earth, they are wounding you. The land should be left untouched: as it was in the Dreamtime when the Ancestors sang the world into existence.'[9]

The Dreaming may also be seen as the 'other' of the Australian awareness, for it embodies the hidden dimension or the shadow, that which is unconscious, strange and unknown to the mode of being which is Australian and white.

It seems that in the very foundations of the Australian experience, the search for meaning is patterned in a meeting of the opposites. For in the Australian context, in the very fabric of life there is an encounter between the ancient and the modern, the black and the white, the dreamer and the rationalist, the nomad and the settler.

Each of the opposites is ambivalent or antagonistic towards and fearful of the other. For it is a frightening thing to encounter the unknown of one's own being. But in that encounter lies the possibility of the birth of a new awareness, a new way of being, and the complementarity without which there cannot be a wholeness.

The Dreaming is the 'being-in-story' of the sacred origins of the Aboriginal Australian, and the Dreaming of contemporary Australians is the entry through symbol and story into their own sacred origins. This implies a capacity to dream, to be attuned to the symbol, to be a weaver of stories, and to awaken to the sacred in all that is.

It is hard, if not impossible for a person of Western culture as we know it, to experience or even imagine what it might be like to live within a total life context that is sacred. The Western mind analyzes and dichotomizes, but to the Australian Aboriginal land, people and person are experienced as one.

The Dreaming means 'In the beginning'. Like the stories of all beginnings the Dreaming mythology was born out of the collective unconscious of a people. It embodies in ever-changing tapestries of symbol their beliefs about the meaning of human existence. The sacred story is woven in patterns of the archetypal nature of human experience, patterns of creation and destruction, patterns of light and darkness, of birth and death, of war and peace. It is out of these primal patterns that the very psyche or soul of a people is formed.

So it was that the child of the Enlightenment who arrived on Australian shores eons of centuries later was ill-equipped to have any understanding of a rich and cohesive spiritual tradition which had been formed out of an ancient people's journey. A highly rationalistic mode confronted an ageless wisdom which had its roots in the timeless and the sacred.

The myth, indeed, is the sacred story of a people, and each of us is a mythmaker. Myth holds in symbol and story the truth of a people in its particularity. But it is also the story of the universal human being. In symbolic language the Dreaming explores what it is to be human and to be one with the Divine. It explores that relationship not only for the Australian Aboriginal, but for the human being.

The myths of any culture, although the language and the symbolic context pertain to that culture, hold in themselves the primal patterns or archetypes which describe how it is to be human. So it is with Greek or Indian myths, with Biblical mythology, and with the Dreaming. In coming to understand the Dreaming, the Australian has a source of wisdom about life and about him or herself that is transcultural, and particularly apt in a land and history that have been shared.

In a small book, recently published, called *Mysteries of the Dreaming*,[10] James Cowan, the Australian poet and novelist who has also lived with Australian Aboriginal tribal people, opens some possible points of entry into these mysteries. And throughout the book he recognizes parallels with other spiritual traditions. He begins by examining the spiritual discipline and psychic power inhering in the formation of the 'karadji', a man of high degree within the Australian Aboriginal community. He was the 'clever' man of the tribe, the one with capacity to 'seize what is imperceptible'. He was noticed by 'the light radiating from his eyes' and the journey of initiation was to lead him to the opening of his 'inner eye'.[11]

The spiritual formation of the karadji was in accord with the most rigorous testing in any spiritual tradition. Such formation required the undergoing of ritual death and rebirth. Many of the experiences of mystical states — ineffability, direct knowing, timelessness, and a profound sense of the unity and indivisibility of all life — were as natural to the Australian Aboriginal people as the air they breathed, and were especially evident in the 'karadji'. In the journey which led him to the opening of his inner eye or the attainment of spiritual insight, he had to spend long periods in solitude and learn the secret lore of the tribe. The entry of crystals into his body imparted to him the capacity to detect and heal sickness in all its forms — physical, mental, psychic and spiritual.

Spiritual power was both recognized and reverenced, and Cowan includes some extraordinary quotations from Australian Aboriginal people describing how they would enter into and experience this mode of deep knowing. An Australian Aboriginal describes the gradual opening of the inner eye in this way: 'He sees and is trained to see further by the "rai" (spirits). In the beginning he is unable to see very far. His sight is still dim. As yet he doesn't know (understand). So the rai, they send a spirit animal or insect out to him. Then his eyes begin to open and he is astonished. That's the way he begins to see further and further.'[12]

Here is a description of the Australian Aboriginal way of entering into sight and visionary experience:

'When you see an old man sitting by himself over there in the camp, do not disturb him, for if you do he will "growl" at you. Do not play near him, because he is sitting down by himself with his thoughts in order to *see*. He is gathering those thoughts so that he can feel and hear. Perhaps he then lies down, getting into a special posture, so that he can *see* while sleeping (meditating). He sees indistinct visions and hears *specific* "persons" (rai/Oruncha) talking to him. He gets up and looks for those he has *seen*, but not seeing them, he lies down again in the prescribed manner, so as to see what he has seen before. He puts his head on the pillow as previously so as to *see* (invoke a vision) as before. Getting up he tells his friends to strengthen that power (known as miwi), a constituent of the quartz crystals within themselves, so that when they lie down they will be able to see and feel (or become aware of) people spirits present, and in that way they will perceive them.'[13]

It is out of this meditative sleeping and seeing that the songlines of the Dreaming are found and expressed.

As the Australian Aboriginal does, each of us must go on our Dream Journey. For as Thomas Merton says 'If we can voyage to the end of the earth and there find ourselves in the Aborigine who most differs from ourselves, we will have made a fruitful pilgrimage.'[14]

The Dream Journey is born out of the wisdom of aboriginality which knows with total immediacy that the land is sacred, and the immanance of spirit in the land forms is that which connects a person to his own soul country. It is a journey of the seasons, an annual return to the original place of the Dreaming. And it is there that the Dreaming goes on. The need to survive and to continually re-enter the rhythm of giving and receiving is a love-song with the land. It is holistically woven in with the celebration and re-living of the primal events of creation. Dance, story-telling and song are the vibrant and living expressions of the sacred significance of each stage of the journey. The Dream Journey is the life-giving re-entry into the creation of the world.

It is, too, a pilgrimage of the soul, both tribal and individual. It is an outer and an inner journey, and the ceremonial aspects are carried out at the sacred sites or 'hot places'. Both ceremonies and dreaming sites are empowered with spirit energy, as is the inner landscape of tribe and person. Rather than being a physical place, it is a state of mind, a spirit awareness, a return to the source.

Nature is 'numen', the vessel of divine power. One of the most potent expressions of deity among Aboriginals throughout Australia is the Rainbow Serpent, the rainbow signifying transfiguration, the meeting of heaven and earth, the throne of the Sky God. In cosmic symbology, the celestial serpent is associated with the rainbow in that it, too, can be a bridge between one world and another. In French, African, Indian and Amerindian symbolism, the rainbow is also a serpent which quenches its thirst in the sea.

The serpent is thus a highly complex and universal symbol. It can be male, female, or self-created. As a killer, it is death and destruction; renewing its skin periodically, it is life and resurrection; coiled, it is equated with the cycles of manifestation. It is solar and lunar, life and death, light and darkness, good and evil, wisdom and blind passion, healing and poison, preserver and destroyer and both spiritual and physical rebirth. It is phallic, the procreative male force, 'the husband of all women', and the presence of a serpent is almost universally associated with pregnancy. It accompanies all female deities and the Great Mother, and is often depicted twining around them or held in their hands. Here it also takes on the feminine characteristics of the secret, enigmatic and intuitional; it is the unpredictable in that it appears and disappears suddenly.[15]

The Rainbow Serpent of the Australian Aboriginals was the matrix of the creative process, moving in the creation of landforms, in the mysterious phenomena of seasonal changes, and in the primal events of the Dreaming. It was the Great Serpent who made the paths for water to flow, and as the Source of Life formed the unique path for the spirit child to be enfleshed. Only the 'clever man' of the tribe could walk across the rainbow bridge and live, for it was he who had power to mediate between the worlds.

The Australian Aboriginal sense of space and time is entirely different from that of the European. There is no word for 'time' in their language, for the experience of the Dreaming awareness is that 'all is always now', and the context is timeless or eternal, or as T. S. Eliot describes it, 'it is where the timeless intersects with time'.[16] We who come from a time sense that is linear may have occasional glimpses or experiences of another time awareness more akin to that of our Australian Aboriginal sisters and brothers.

We are accustomed to space that has clear definition, and is frequently broken by lines and shapes. We would perhaps consider that we had mastered space in the miracles of aviation and space exploration. Whatever the way we experience ourselves in space, there is a sense of control and mastery in the ways we organize and relate to our space.

Cowan draws attention to the contrasting way in which Australian Aboriginal people inhabit space. For them, there are no parameters, for they inhabit the earth as universe, and the universe itself is home. The sense of space is defined out of a finely tuned sensory and intuitive awareness, as it were, a quivering attentiveness which is amazingly accurate, and does not need the protective coverings of strong walls or clothes.[17]

The particular pattern of his spirit-being is his totem, and his is the spirit energy of emu, kangaroo, sea-eagle, dingo or lizard. The totem is and mirrors the very pattern of his soul and life energy. The sacred is distilled, too, in a particular way in the 'churinga' which embodies in its markings the events of the Dreaming and emanates spiritual power.

We are exploring here a way of being that many of us know little about, although we may know some of the words. Our way of life does not easily let us enter into it. This way of being, the Australian Aboriginal artist and writer, Miriam Rose, described as 'Dadirri — the deep spring of inner, deep listening and quiet still awareness' that is within us all. As she sees it, this is the gift the Aboriginal people have for us if we are open to receive.[18]

The last chapter of Cowan's *Mysteries of the Dreaming* is entitled 'Towards a New Dreaming'. Cowan claims that if Australian Aboriginal culture is to survive at all, then the Dreaming as a metaphysical statement must be honored. For, as he says, the Dreaming is the *raison d'etre* of Aboriginal culture, and without it the culture will die.

The implications are many, and in his opinion include the necessity of a radical change of awareness in many Australians; the full restoration of their sacred land sites to the Australian Aboriginal people; and total freedom to live the Dreaming unmolested.

He concludes: 'The Dreaming still exists. The pure asceticism of nature as an attainable condition within every one of us is possible if we listen to what the Aborigine is saying to us. Reestablishing our links with totems, making our own Dream Journeys, listening to the voice of our own Dreaming and acknowledging our ancestors as being primordially present, is the beginning of the process of renewal.'[19]

The songs are still being sung and the songlines still being travelled, in the past by Australian Aboriginal people and in the present and future by all Australians. Let us honor the hope in the songlines by concluding with a sad song of the now, sung by the Australian Aboriginal poet Oodgeroo of the tribe Noonuccal (formerly Kath Walker):[20]

WE ARE GOING

They came into the little town
a semi-naked band subdued and silent,
All that remained of their tribe.
They came here to the place of their old bora ground
Where now the many white men hurry about like ants.

Notice of estate agent reads: 'Rubbish May Be Tipped
Here'.
Now it half covers the traces of the old bora ring.
They sit and are confused, they cannot say their thoughts:
'We are as strangers here now, but the white tribe are the
strangers.
We belong here, we are of the old ways.
We are the old sacred ceremonies, the laws of the elders.
We are the wonder tales of Dream Time, the tribal legends
told.
We are the past, the hunts and the laughing games, the
wandering camp fires.
We are the lightning-bolt over Gaphembah Hill.
Quick and terrible,
And the Thunderer after him, that loud fellow.
We are the quiet daybreak paling the dark lagoon.
We are the shadow-ghosts creeping back as campfires burn
low.
We are nature and the past, all the old ways.
Gone now and scattered.
The scrubs are gone, the hunting and the laughter.
The eagle is gone, the emu and the kangaroo are gone from
this place.
The bora ring is gone.
The corroboree is gone.
And we are going.'

NOTES

1. Pownall, E., *Australian Pioneer Women*, V. O'Neil, Australia,
   1989.
2. Modjeska, D., *Inner Cities*, Penguin, 1989.
3. Blainey, G., *A Land Half Won*, Macmillan, Melbourne, 1980.
4. Hughes, R., *The Fatal Shore*, Pan Books, Sydney, 1988.
5. Morgan, S., *My Place*, Fremantle Arts Centre Press, WA, 1987.
6. Clarke, M., *The Puzzle of Childhood*, Penguin, 1990.
7. Chatwin, B., *The Songlines*, Picador, London, 1988, p 314.
8. Eliot, T. S., *Four Quartets*, Faber & Faber, mcmlix, p 314.
9. Chatwin, B., op. cit, p 13.

10. Cowan, J., *Mysteries of the Dreaming*, Prism Press, Bridport, UK, 1989, pp 5–20.
11. Op. cit, Chapter 1.
12. Op. cit, p 12.
13. Op. cit, p 13.
14. Op. cit, p 43.
15. Cooper, J. C., *An Illustrated Encyclopaedia of Traditional Symbols*, Thames & Hudson, 1984.
16. Eliot, T. S., op. cit, p 44.
17. Cowan, J., op. cit, Chapter 6.
18. Ungunnmerr-Baumann, M. R., *Dadirri*; Address: International Liturgy Assembly, Hobart, Dec 1987.
19. Cowan J., op. cit, pp 125–6.
20. Oodgeroo of the tribe Noonuccal (formerly Kath Walker), "We Are Going", *My People*, Jacaranda Press, Australia, 1964, p 78.

An Aboriginal Response

EDDIE KNEEBONE
(Interviewed by C. Hammond, Editor)

C. H.   *How would you describe Aboriginal spirituality — the Dreamtime — to someone unfamiliar with it?*

E. K.   How can I answer that in a few moments?... But I'll do my best.

Aboriginal spirituality is the belief and the feeling within yourself that allows you to become a part of the whole environment around you — not the built environment, but the natural environment... Birth, life and death are all a part of it, and you welcome each.

Aboriginal spirituality is the belief that all objects are living and share the same soul or spirit that Aboriginals share. Therefore all Aboriginals have a kinship with the environment. The soul or spirit is common — only the shape is different, but no less important.

Aboriginal spirituality is the belief that the soul or spirit will continue on after our physical form has passed away through death. The spirit will return to the Dreamtime from where it came, it will carry out memories to the Dreamtime and eventually it will return again through birth, either as a human or an animal or even trees and rocks. The shape is not important because everything is equal and shares the same soul or spirit from the Dreamtime.

Aboriginal spirituality is not the equal of the European ideology of reincarnation. The Dreamtime is there with them, it is not a long way away. The Dreamtime is the environment that the Aboriginal lived in, and it still exists today, all around us.

C. H.   *Where does an Aboriginal go to worship?*

E. K.   Aboriginals *don't go anywhere* to worship, because everything around them is alive and they are totally in touch, constantly with the Dreamtime, or the place of the spirits. But it's not the spirit world of the Europeans. It is everything that is living around them, that shares that common soul or spirit. It includes the entire environment. The Aboriginals didn't worship in the same context as Europeans do, but they did have special places for ceremonies that were necessary for the continuation of Aboriginal culture and teachings to the younger ones as they became older. These places are known as sacred places, or sites. These areas are where the Dreamtime spirits dwell and are the strongest.

C. H.   *Is there a similarity here with the American Indian's concept of the Great Spirit and the lesser spirits — or the Christian concept of the Creator and the Angels?*

E. K.   Not in that context. Certainly there is the Creator spirit, and then from there the Creator spirit gave life. The life that he gave was also the spirit, strong enough to make everything live and feel, and to continue flowing through people and the environment.

Within Christianity there is God the Creator and the Angels, an army of beings, or spirits — for one reason or another. In addition to that there is the power of God, or the spirit that allows things to live. Aboriginal belief is similar to that, except that there is no multitude of angels or spirits. Just the Creator spirit and the Dreamtime spirits that were created by the Creator spirit, and the spirit or soul, the life force that is common in all living things, flows from the Dreamtime and the Creator spirit through the environment to the

Aborigines and back to the Dreamtime.

C. H.   *What is Aboriginal worship like? Is it practiced in the community, or mainly alone? Are there certain rituals you consider part of your spirituality and worship?*

E. K.   Again, Aboriginals do not go to worship the spirit as Europeans would go to church, to pay homage to God, to worship him, to talk to him. For the Aboriginals, the spirit is ever present and they are very aware of that presence. At certain times, during ceremonies and initiations of the young people, moving from one period of their lives to the next, they were taken to the special places or sacred sites where the spirit was the strongest. This could be seen as a form of worship, but not so, it was more of an introduction to the spirits of the Dreamtime rather than worship. Before the ceremonies take place, there are songs and chantings, which could be called religious. In a pleasant way the Aborigines invite the Dreamtime Spirit from the dwelling place to come out and join in the ceremony that is happening there. They entice the spirit out in a friendly manner, not to harm them, but to make the person or persons who are going through the ceremonies stronger.

Without the chanting and the sacred songs, the spirit will not come out. If they go to the site without that in their minds, they believe that the spirit will become angry with them. So they go there and invite the spirit to join them through chanting.

If there are rock paintings (almost all sacred sites had paintings), an indication that the spirit is stronger in that place, the Aboriginals would repaint the paintings, freshen them up—bringing them alive with a fresh coat of paint or ochre. The painting would be accompanied with songs and chantings, inviting the spirit: 'come out and join us in this ceremony!'

C. H.   *How do you see the relationship of soul and body?*

E. K.   I see our bodies as a container. When we are at peace with ourselves, all the things that we fill the container will fit. Only the good things fit. When they fit, there is harmony. When the container of the world is empty, and we try to fill it with the wrong things, there are sharp edges, there are misfits; things do not meld; there are empty spaces, holes. The container is not full. This creates an imbalance, and that makes us unhappy, ill and hungry for something to fill those spaces. That's how I see our bodies. There should be a balance. Those things that we put into our bodies and minds should fit equally and evenly. If we can do that then we will be in harmony not only within ourselves but with the environment as well.

C. H.   *What do you think we Europeans or Australians most need to take from Aboriginal spirituality?*

E. K.   They need to learn to share. They have taken everything else (said with a good-natured chuckle) but they can't take Aboriginal spirituality without sharing. We, as Aboriginals, have to remember our spirituality and share as well, especially with those who would take everything. The Aboriginals can never lose their spirituality if they freely share it. Europeans and Aboriginals alike have to learn together to share, that is the one common factor that we all need, and can gain from Aboriginal spirituality.

C. H.   *What have you, as an Aboriginal, found in Matthew Fox, in Creation Spirituality, that you haven't found in other Christian groups?*

E. K.   I found that there was an opening up there. It felt as if a door had been opened and light was shining through. I felt that something was being offered which I had not experienced anywhere else. For the first time, instead of going to look for someone else to fill the need in my life, I realized that I was the one who could fill that need. Because of this realization from being here I can now go out and see the world differently, I am able to accept my place in it better, I have a clearer understanding of it.

One of the things I have heard Matthew Fox say was that we can look at ourselves, we don't need anybody else to tell us which way to go. If we look within ourselves and find out why we are stumbling and learn to stand, we can learn to walk. If we can become at peace with ourselves, with our souls, then we can go and tell others how we did it.

So I felt for the first time that I can find peace of heart. What Matthew Fox is saying makes sense, it shows a lot of understanding.

I have found peace of heart — but not in a building. I was told to 'Go to church, that is where you will find God, inside the church'. I have also realized that man created the buildings that he calls churches, God created the world. If I look for God then it will be in the environment that he built.

C. H.   *What aspects of Creation Spirituality are you most comfortable with? What aspect seems to tie in best with the Dreamtime?*

E. K.   The aspect of being at one with the universe — not just the little piece of land that we stand on, not simply the environment around us, nor the country that we live in — but the universe. It is included in our lives. It is a part of us.

During the daytime we can look outside and we see trees, birds, rivers, the wind in the clouds and the sunshine. This is the environment that is revealed during the daylight hours, that we take for granted. But at night the other half of our environment is revealed — the universe. Every clear night we can look up and see millions of stars. That is also a part of our lives. It is an important part of our lives that we forget about and don't include in our way of thinking.

In Aboriginal spirituality, however, it certainly was included.

We look up and see the stars shining above and we say: 'They are the bright suns and around them there are planets—possibly with people that we will never see.' The Aboriginals looked up at night and they didn't see the stars—they never *saw* stars. They only saw the campfires of their ancestors on their journey. The bright stars were the ancestors who were not long gone; the dimmer stars were the ancestors further on the journey.

They imagined that the ancestors sitting around their campfires were looking back and seeing the campfires of the living, physical Aboriginals at their own campsites. The Aboriginals looked up and really believed that their eyes could meet.

So for me, Creation Spirituality, as Matthew Fox talks about it, is like the Dreamtime in the way that it brings the entire cosmos into our lives, making it a part of us, and us, a part of if.